100 GREAT STIR-FRIES

KAY FAIRFAX

PHOTOGRAPHS BY
ROBIN MATTHEWS

WEIDENFELD
& NICOLSON
LONDON

CONTENTS

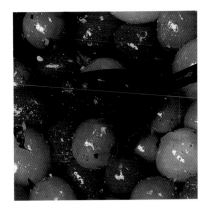

THE STORECUPBOARD

Many of these ingredients are not essential items normally found in your storecupboard, and several may be new to you.
But once you have mastered the simple art of stir-frying you will want to experiment and become more adventurous
with varied flavours and textures. Most stir-fry recipes use the best fresh ingredients with large amounts of seasonal vegetables and
fruit, smaller portions of lean meat, poultry, fish and seafood. So if you have a selection of sauces, spices, nuts, rice and noodles in the
cupboard already, you can create a new inspired taste sensation in less than one hour from arriving home to sitting down to a
fabulous meal. Remember that the list here is only a guide, and should be tailored to suit your own requirements.

SPICES
Whole Black Peppercorns, Whole Red Peppercorns, Sea Salt, Chinese Five Spice

DRY GOODS
Cornflour, Stockcubes (Chicken, Beef, Fish and Vegetable), Brown Sugar, Dried Chinese Mushrooms, Dried Citrus Peel

CANNED GOODS
Water Chestnuts, Bamboo Shoots, Pineapple

OIL AND VINEGAR
White Wine Vinegar, Groundnut Oil (also known as Peanut Oil), Sesame Oil, Walnut Oil, Hazelnut Oil, Macadamia Nut Oil, Pistachio Oil

NUTS AND SEEDS
Sesame Seeds, Pine Nuts, Unsalted Peanuts, Unsalted Cashew Nuts, Almonds (whole and flaked), Whole Walnuts, Whole Hazelnuts, Pecan Nuts, Macadamia Nuts

NOODLES
Bean Thread Noodles (Clear and Transparent), Rice Noodles (Opaque or Clear White), Soft Fresh Noodles, Chinese Egg Noodles (Rounded not Flat), Rice Vermicelli

RICE
Long Grain White Rice, Brown Rice, Red Camargue Rice

SOY SAUCE
Made from fermented soy beans, flour and water. Light Soy is paler in colour and saltier than the dark variety and is used more in the cooking of white meats. Dark Soy is aged longer than the paler variety. It is thicker, darker, more strongly flavoured and is used in the cooking of red meats.

FLAVOURINGS
Pale Dry Sherry, Shaoxing Wine

OYSTER SAUCE
A thick, rich brown sauce made from oysters cooked in brine and soy sauce. It does not have a strong fishy taste. Once opened it is best kept in the fridge.

FISH SAUCE
A thin, clear salty sauce with a strong smell and flavour. Once opened it is best kept in the fridge.

HOISIN SAUCE (CHINESE BARBECUE SAUCE)
A thick, dark, sweet and spicy sauce made from soy beans. Once opened it is best kept in the fridge.

CHILLI SAUCE
Made from hot chillis, it is bright red and HOT so use sparingly or dilute with a little hot water if it is too strong. Use according to personal taste.

CHILLI BEAN SAUCE
A dark, thick, spicy sauce which can vary from mild to very hot, so use sparingly until you find the degree of "heat" you enjoy.

SWEET CHILLI SAUCE
A sweet sauce usually with the seeds left in.

BLACK BEAN SAUCE
A smooth sauce made from fermented soy beans.

YELLOW BEAN SAUCE
This sauce is available in two varieties: whole beans or crushed beans. It is a thick, salty, spicy sauce.

SWEET AND SOUR SAUCE
Combines well with meat, chicken, fish and vegetables. A deep, orangy-red, made from red peppers, tomatoes, vinegar, garlic and ginger. Not too hot or spicy.

TAMARIND SAUCE
A thick. brown and tangy sauce with a slightly acid flavour, but not bitter.

TERIYAKI SAUCE
Similar to Japanese Soy Sauce.

PESTO SAUCE
This sauce is a wonderful green colour and is made from fresh basil, pine nuts, garlic, olive oil, salt and freshly ground black pepper.

TOMATO SAUCE
No explanation needed but make sure you buy a good quality sauce.

WORCESTERSHIRE SAUCE
Only the original Lea and Perrins will do.

WOKS AND STIR-FRY PANS

It is best to buy a wok that is at least 30-35cm/12-14in in diameter because it is much easier to toss food around in a large pan than a small one. The rounded-bottom woks can only be used on gas, but there are now many flat-bottomed designs to use on all fuel surfaces, so check carefully before buying. The time of cooking will vary depending on which pan or wok you use, so you may have to slightly adjust the cooking times given in the recipes to suit your wok or pan.

CARBON STEEL WOK

This is not an expensive item to buy and is much superior to the stainless steel or aluminum woks. It can take high heat without burning itself or the food. Remember it must be seasoned before using the first time.

STAINLESS STEEL/ALUMINiUM/CAST IRON

I do not recommend stainless steel or aluminium woks as I find they burn and smoke on high temperatures, and I find the cast iron too heavy to handle easily.

NON-STICK

These are suitable for stir-frying, but they cannot take as high a temperature as carbon steel, and remember not to use metal utensils or scourers as they will damage the non-stick coating. The best of the non-stick surfaces I have found is the tefal-coated variety.

FLAT-BOTTOMED HIGH-SIDED PAN

Any flat-bottomed, high-sided pan can be used to stir-fry, but make sure the handle is long and does not become too hot to hold during cooking. The high sides make it easier to toss the ingredients.

SEASONING THE WOK

Before using a wok for the first time it must be properly seasoned. First scrub the inside with a non-abrasive cleaner to remove any protective machine oil left on by the manufacturer, and dry well. Place the wok on the stove and, when warm and completely dry, coat the inside surface with vegetable oil (not olive oil). When the oil begins to smoke, remove the wok from the heat and allow it to cool. Using kitchen paper, wipe off all the excess oil. The paper will blacken. Repeat this oiling process 2 or 3 times or until the kitchen paper wipes clean.

This process ensures the wok is properly seasoned and will not rust or burn. Always make sure the wok is completely dry after use and it is advisable to wipe the surface with a small amount of vegetable oil before storing. Never scrub the wok again, it should only be washed in hot water and wiped dry.

UTENSILS

Many of the following utensils may already be in your kitchen, but for successful stir-frying it is well worth investing in a few special pieces of equipment: a good-quality wok, very sharp kinves and a slotted spoon.

PEPPER GRINDER

This is used in most recipes, so choose a good-quality one that will coarsely grind the peppercorns and not just crush them into powder.

CHOPPING BOARDS

Wooden ones will prevent the work surface from being damaged and scratched. The plastic or white acrylic ones should be used when chopping coriander, garlic or any foods with a strong smell.

SHARP KNIVES

Stir-frying entails a great deal of chopping and slicing, so have a good selection of knives and keep them really sharp.

MINI CLEAVER

Buy a good quality stainless-steel mini cleaver. Once you become familiar with this traditional Chinese utensil you can use it to prepare everything, from chopping meat, crushing garlic to slicing vegetables.

MINI WIRE WHISK

This is a great help for combining liquid and cornflour before adding to the wok, and helps to ensure no lumps occur in the sauce.

LONG-HANDLED METAL SLOTTED SPOON

Very useful in the removal of meat from the pan when cooking in batches.

BRASS WIRE SKIMMER

This is a traditional utensil used in wok cooking, but a long-handled slotted spoon is just as effective.

STAINLESS-STEEL STRAINER

Used for draining rice or noodles. I prefer the simple long-handled type.

STIFF SPLIT-BAMBOO BRUSH

A traditional brush used to clean the wok, but an ordinary soft plastic washing up brush is just as good.

PLASTIC SPATULA

This is a great for scraping out the last remains from the bowl or jug.

LONG-HANDLED STAINLESS-STEEL WOK SPATULA

This is a long-handled curved metal spatula made for tossing meat and vegetables. It is shaped to the curve of the sides of the wok. It is easy to use, but only on carbon-steel surfaces, not on non-stick or tefal-coated surfaces.

MEASURING JUGS

Invest in two or three different sized glass jugs with both metric and imperial measurements. A small one is very useful to combine lesser amounts, and is the most effective means of adding liquid to the pan, thus leaving one hand free to continue stirring.

MEASURING SPOONS

Most amounts used in sti- frying are small, so a variety of different sized spoons is very useful.

MIXING BOWLS

I prefer heavy glass bowls. These are especially useful for marinating as well as for mixing the liquids.

GARLIC CRUSHER

Buy a good-quality one that is easy to clean, as this utensil is used many times in stir-fry recipes.

JULIENNE CUTTER

This is very useful for making uniform sized thin vegetable sticks. Ideal for carrots and courgettes.

KITCHEN SCISSORS

Many people find it easier to snip parsley, chives and other herbs with sharp scissors rather than with a knife.

DOUBLE-HANDLED CHOPPER/HACHOIR KNIFE/ROSTFREI

This is my favourite utensil for chopping herbs, and I find it much quicker than other methods.

LONG-HANDLED WOODEN SPATULA

This resembles a flat salad server, and is a must for tossing the food in a wok or pan. Most importantly they are not abrasive on non-stick or tefal-coated pans.

KITCHEN SCALES

Invest in a good-quality set of scales that have both imperial and metric measurements. They save a great deal of guesswork and ensure you have the correct amounts required for the recipe.

VEGETABLE PEELER

There are various designs of vegetable peelers on the market, so choose the one you are most comfortable with. An important utensil for preparing the vegetables and for making the citrus peel.

THE RECIPES

MEAT & POULTRY

Always buy the best fresh, lean cuts of meat and poultry available. As stir-fry recipes use much smaller proportions of meat to vegetables this is not an extravagance and makes all the difference to the end result. You can interchange cuts of meat and poultry for most of the recipes in this chapter.

Beef, Lettuce and Noodles

This combination noodle soup is a great family dish. You can use any type of noodle in this recipe except vermicelli. Serves 4.

FOR THE MARINADE

1 tsp salt
Pinch of brown sugar
45ml/3 tbsp light soy sauce
2 tsp pale dry sherry
30ml/2 tbsp sesame oil
30ml/2 tbsp water

450g/1lb beef fillet, cut into 5mm/ ¼in thick slices
5 turns of freshly ground black pepper
2 garlic cloves, sliced
1 tsp cornflour

250g/9oz Chinese egg noodles
15ml/1 tbsp sesame seeds
15ml/1 tbsp groundnut oil
1 chilli, deseeded and finely sliced
200ml/7fl oz water
1 little gem or iceberg lettuce, or Chinese leaves
2 spring onions, sliced

In a large bowl, combine the ingredients for the marinade and add the beef. Leave this for 15-20 minutes. Now cook the noodles as directed on the packet. Drain well, toss with the sesame seeds and set aside.

Heat the wok, add the groundnut oil and, when the oil is very hot and begins to smoke, add the beef, the marinade itself, the chilli and the garlic. Stir for 3-4 minutes. With a slotted spoon, remove the beef and set this aside, keeping it hot. Add the water to the marinade in the wok and bring this to a simmer. Add the lettuce or Chinese leaves and stir for 1 minute. Remove and arrange it on top of noodles. Return the beef to the wok with the spring onions and stir it for 1 minute to reheat. Remove it and arrange it on top of the noodles and lettuce. Pour the remaining soup from the wok over the noodles if desired.

Pork and Lychee Curry

This is a delicious combination of flavours and textures with the lychees adding extra interest. Serve with white rice. Serves 4.

450g/1lb pork, cut into bite-size chunks
65g/2 ½oz plain flour
45ml/3 tbsp groundnut oil
1-2 tbsp green curry paste
400ml/14fl oz coconut milk

35ml/1fl oz lychee syrup
1 chilli, deseeded and finely chopped
2 bay leaves
15ml/1 tbsp fish sauce
425g/15oz tin of lychees

Toss the pork pieces in the flour and shake off any excess.

Heat the wok, add the groundnut oil and, when the oil is very hot and begins to smoke, add the pork pieces and stir for 3-4 minutes or until golden brown. Remove them and rest on kitchen paper. Wipe out the wok to remove any remaining oil.

Reheat the wok, adding the curry paste. Mash this for ½ minute before adding the coconut milk and lychee syrup, stir well. Bring the liquid to a simmer, then add the chilli, bay leaves and fish sauce, stirring for 2 minutes. Add the pork and lychees, letting everything simmer for a few more minutes. Remove the bay leaves before serving.

Chicken Livers and Bacon

This is a marvellous starter or a light luncheon dish. Serve it on a bed of steamed white rice and sprinkle it with chive flowers. Serves 4.

450g/1lb chicken livers, cleaned and chopped
15ml/1 tbsp pale dry sherry
2 tsp cornflour
2 tsp water

15ml/1 tbsp groundnut oil
1 onion, finely chopped
3 rashers lean bacon, finely chopped
1 tbsp fresh chives, chopped
Freshly ground black pepper

Soak the livers in a bowl of boiling water, drain them and repeat this process 2-3 times. (This will eliminate any bitterness.) Drain well and pat dry with kitchen paper.

In a small jug, combine the sherry, cornflour and water. Heat the wok, add the groundnut oil and, when the oil is very hot and begins to smoke, add the onion and bacon and stir for 1 minute. Add the livers and stir for 1 minute. Remove the wok from the heat and stir in the cornflour mixture. Return the wok to the heat and stir for 1 minute. Add the chopped chives and stir for ½ minute. Season with black pepper to taste.

Right: Beef, Lettuce and Noodles

DUCK AND ORANGE

Duck and orange make a classic – and favourite – combination. This super-quick dish has the extra crunch of mangetout. Serves 4.

250g/9oz white long grain rice	2 tsp pale dry sherry
2 tsp orange rind, grated or finely shredded	2 oranges
450g/1lb duck breast, sliced into	1 tbsp honey
1cm/½in wide pieces	45ml/3 tbsp boiling water
½ tsp salt	15ml/1 tbsp groundnut oil
5 turns of freshly ground black pepper	75g/3oz mangetout, trimmed
1 tsp cornflour	

Cook the rice with 1 tsp of the orange rind in the cooking water. Drain it well and keep hot. Marinate the duck slices in salt, pepper, cornflour, 1 tsp orange rind and 1 tsp sherry for 15 minutes. Peel the oranges and remove the skin from around the segments. Place these in a separate bowl with 1 tsp sherry and mix well. In another small bowl, mix together the honey and boiling water, stirring to dissolve the honey. With a slotted spoon, remove the duck pieces from the marinade and brush them with the honey and water mixture. Heat the wok, add the groundnut oil and, when the oil is very hot and begins to smoke, add the duck along with the marinade and stir for 3 minutes. Add the oranges and mangetout and stir for 2-3 minutes. Remove from the heat and serve on a bed of hot rice.

VEAL, MUSHROOMS AND GARLIC

The ginger and coriander give a hint of the Orient to this dish and perfectly complement the veal. Serves 4.

15ml/1 tbsp pale dry sherry	450g/1lb veal, thinly sliced
1 tsp light soy sauce	200g/7oz courgettes, sliced diagonally
½ tsp cornflour	150g/5oz button mushrooms, sliced
30ml/2 tbsp groundnut oil	1 tbsp fresh coriander, chopped
1 garlic clove, finely chopped	Freshly ground black pepper
1 tsp fresh ginger, grated	

In a small jug, combine the sherry, soy sauce and cornflour.

Heat the wok, add the groundnut oil and, when the oil is very hot and begins to smoke, add the garlic and ginger and stir for ½ minute. Add the veal and stir for 3-4 minutes until it is browned and tender. With a slotted spoon, remove the veal from the wok and set aside.

Return the wok to the heat, add the courgettes and stir for 2 minutes, add the mushrooms and stir for 1 minute. Add the cornflour mixture and stir for 1 minute. Return the veal to the wok and stir for 1 minute or until the vegetables are cooked but still crisp. Stir through the fresh coriander and finish off with freshly ground black pepper.

NAVARIN LAMB

Great at any time of year, this makes a particularly good summer lunch when served with a green salad. Serves 4.

15ml/1 tbsp dry sherry	250g/9oz long grain white rice, pre-cooked
Finely shredded rind of 1 lemon	and cooled
1 tsp caster sugar	3 spring onions, finely chopped diagonally
15ml/1 tbsp groundnut oil	50g/2oz sultanas
1 garlic clove, crushed	50g/2oz cashew nuts
1 tsp fresh ginger, grated	Salt
450g/1lb lean lamb fillet, cut into	Freshly ground black pepper
thin strips	2 tsp walnut oil

In a small jug, combine the sherry, lemon rind and sugar. Set aside.

Heat the wok, add the groundnut oil and, when the oil is very hot and begins to smoke, add the garlic and ginger. Stir for ½ minute. Add the lamb and stir for 3-4 minutes or until well browned. Add the sherry mixture. Stir for 1 minute. Add the rice and stir for 2-3 minutes until rice is hot. Add the spring onions and stir for 1 minute. Add the sultanas and cashew nuts, and season with salt and pepper to taste. Finally, add the walnut oil and stir for ½ minute.

SPICY MANGO BEEF

The combination of fresh mango and pickle makes this beef very special. It's best made when mangoes are in season but you can still substitute tinned ones successfully. Serves 4.

450g/1lb fillet or rump steak,	2 fresh mangoes, peeled and cut into
cut into strips	large chunks
4 tbsp mango pickle	Salt
15ml/1 tbsp groundnut oil	Freshly ground black pepper

Marinate the sliced beef in the mango pickle for 15 minutes.

Heat the wok, add the groundnut oil and, when the oil is very hot and begins to smoke, add the beef and stir for 3-4 minutes. Remove any excess pickle from the wok and add the fresh mango pieces. Stir gently for 1-2 minutes, making sure not to break up the mango pieces. Season with salt and pepper to taste.

Right: Duck and Orange

LAMB, SUGARSNAPS AND MINT

The slightly sweet taste of the mint and the tang of the coriander does wonders for the flavour of the lamb in this recipe. Serves 4.

30ml/2 tbsp soy sauce	2 garlic cloves, crushed
30ml/2 tbsp water	2 tsp fresh ginger, grated
2 tsp cornflour	50g/2oz pine nuts, roasted
1 level tbsp fresh coriander, chopped	200g/7oz sugarsnaps, trimmed
30ml/2 tbsp groundnut oil	3 sprigs fresh mint, chopped
450g/1lb lean lamb fillet, sliced	2 tsp sesame oil

In a small jug, mix together the soy sauce, water, cornflour and half the chopped coriander.

Heat the wok, add the groundnut oil and, when the oil is very hot and begins to smoke, add the lamb and stir for 2-3 minutes or until it is browned. Add the garlic, ginger and half the nuts, stirring for 1 minute. Add the sugarsnaps, the remaining coriander and the mint. Stir for 2 minutes. Remove the wok from the heat and stir in the soy sauce mixture. Return the wok to the heat and stir for a further 2 minutes. Add the sesame oil and stir for 1 minute. Sprinkle with the remaining pine nuts and serve.

SWEET AND SOUR PORK

Truly a classic, this is best served with white rice. Serves 4.

15ml/1 tbsp light soy sauce	2 tsp fresh ginger, grated
1 tbsp brown sugar	450g/1lb lean pork fillet, cut into strips
45ml/3 tbsp malt or sherry vinegar	2 small carrots, thinly sliced diagonally
85ml/3fl oz pineapple juice	1 medium-sized onion, finely chopped
1 tbsp cornflour	1 medium-sized green pepper, deseeded and
30ml/2 tbsp groundnut oil	cut into strips
1 garlic clove, crushed	2 tbsp pineapple pieces

In a jug, combine the soy sauce, brown sugar, vinegar, pineapple juice and cornflour. Mix well.

Heat the wok, add the groundnut oil and, when the oil is very hot and begins to smoke, add the garlic and ginger. Stir for ½ minute. Add the pork and stir for 3-4 minutes until the pork is well browned. With a slotted spoon, remove the pork and set aside in a warm place.

Reheat the wok and add the carrots and onion. Stir for 1 minute. Add the green pepper and stir for 2-3 minutes until the vegetables are tender but still crisp. Add the cornflour mixture and stir for 2 minutes. Return the pork to the wok and stir for 2 minutes or until hot. Finally add the pineapple pieces and stir for 2 minutes.

CALVES LIVER AND MUSHROOMS

When cooking liver, never add salt until the end as it will toughen it. This is delicious served with red Camargue rice or with sliced boiled potatoes. Serves 4.

2 tbsp plain flour	1 white onion, sliced into thin rings
Freshly ground black pepper	2 tsp sweet Hungarian paprika
450g/1lb calves liver, sliced into	300g/11oz chanterelle or button
2.5cm/1in strips	mushrooms, sliced
15ml/1 tbsp groundnut oil	120-250ml/4-8fl oz beef stock

Season the flour with black pepper and coat the strips of liver with the seasoned flour, shaking off any excess. Heat the wok, add the groundnut oil and, when the oil is very hot and begins to smoke, add the onion and liver and stir for 1 minute or until the liver is browned. Add the paprika and stir for 1 minute. Add the mushrooms and stir for 1 minute. Add the stock and stir until the sauce thickens.

DUCK AND NOODLES IN SOUP

This is a wonderful way to serve duck and the crackling is worth fighting over! It is best made with fresh duck in season but a frozen bird will taste good too. Serves 4.

400g/14oz duck breast, skinned and	9 thin slices peeled fresh ginger
thinly sliced into 5mm/¼in strips	1 red chilli, deseeded and thinly sliced
(reserve the skin)	500ml/17fl oz water
15ml/1 tbsp groundnut oil	200g/7oz choi sum, chopped
1 spring onion, finely chopped	250g/9oz Chinese egg noodles

FOR THE MARINADE	
½ tsp salt	½ tsp cornflour
½ tsp brown sugar	25ml/1½ tbsp water
15ml/1 tbsp light soy sauce	15ml/1 tbsp groundnut oil
1 tsp pale dry sherry	15ml/1 tbsp sesame oil
5 turns of freshly ground black pepper	

In a large bowl, marinate the duck slices in the salt, sugar, soy sauce, sherry, pepper, cornflour and water for 15 minutes. Add the groundnut oil and sesame oil to the marinade and let it stand for a further 5 minutes.

Heat the wok, add the groundnut oil and, when the oil is very hot and begins to smoke, add the duck skin and stir for 2-3 minutes until golden brown and crisp. With a slotted spoon, remove the skin from the wok and drain it on kitchen paper. Wipe out the wok to remove the excess oil. Reheat the wok, add the duck and marinade, spring onion, ginger and chilli. Stir for 3-4 minutes or until the duck is cooked. With a slotted spoon, remove the duck and set aside in a warm place. Add the water to the wok and bring it to the boil. Add the choi sum and noodles and stir for 1 minute. Return the duck to the wok and stir for 1 minute. Divide into four portions and serve with duck skin crackling on top.

Above: Garlic Lamb with Rosemary

GARLIC LAMB WITH ROSEMARY

Garlic and rosemary are a classic combination with lamb, but the addition of Pernod and the rosemary oil makes this dish extra special. It is delicious served with herbed rice and a green salad. Serves 4.

2 tsp Pernod
2 tsp water
1 tsp cornflour
30ml/2 tbsp groundnut oil
200g/7oz courgettes, thinly sliced
2 garlic cloves, finely chopped
450g/1lb lean lamb fillet, sliced across
the grain into 1cm/½in thick rounds

3 large sprigs rosemary
Salt
Freshly ground black or red peppercorns
1 tsp rosemary oil
1 tbsp grated lemon rind

In a small jug, combine the Pernod, water and cornflour. Heat the wok, add 1 tbsp of the groundnut oil and, when the oil is very hot and begins to smoke, add the courgettes and stir for 3–5 minutes until well browned. Transfer to a plate and set aside. Wipe the wok clean, add the remaining oil and when it is hot, add the garlic and stir for ½ minute. Add the lamb and rosemary and stir for 3 minutes or until the lamb is browned. Add the cornflour mixture and stir for 1 minute. Remove the rosemary and add salt and pepper to taste. Stir for 1 minute. Finally add the rosemary oil and lemon rind and stir for 1 minute. Serve the lamb on rice, topped with the courgettes.

CURRIED NOODLES AND QUAILS EGGS

The quails eggs add an unusual and distinctive flavour to this dish. Use any type of noodle except vermicelli. Serves 4.

12 quails eggs
250g/9oz Chinese egg noodles
450g/1lb pork fillet, cut into cubes
65g/2½oz plain flour
45ml/3 tbsp groundnut oil

200g/7oz asparagus, cut into 3cm/1¼in
lengths
4 tsp curry powder
250ml/8fl oz coconut milk
4 sprigs fresh coriander

Boil the quails eggs for 3 minutes, remove them from the pan immediately and run them under cold water. Allow them to cool before peeling off the shells.

Cook the noodles as directed on the packet. Drain and set aside.

Toss the pork pieces in the flour, removing any excess once coated. Heat the wok, add the groundnut oil and, when the oil is very hot and begins to smoke, add the pork and asparagus. Stir for 2-3 minutes. With a slotted spoon, remove the asparagus and set aside in a warm place. Continue to stir the pork for 2-3 minutes or until golden brown. Remove it from the wok and pat dry with kitchen paper.

Wipe out the remaining oil from the wok. Reheat the wok to a medium temperature and add the curry powder and coconut milk. Stir for 1 minute. Add the quails eggs, asparagus and pork and stir for 1-2 minutes. Add the noodles and stir for 1 minute. Serve garnished with the coriander.

HONEYED PORK

The combination of honey, ginger and sesame seeds creates a delicious sweet and sour taste. This dish is best served with plain white rice and a green salad. Serves 4.

30ml/2 tbsp honey
30ml/2 tbsp light soy sauce
2 tsp Worcestershire sauce
15ml/1 tbsp pale dry sherry
1 tsp cornflour
15ml/1 tbsp groundnut oil

1 garlic clove, crushed or finely chopped
1 tsp fresh ginger, grated
450g/1lb lean pork, sliced into strips
2 spring onions, thinly sliced diagonally
2 tbsp sesame seeds, roasted
1 tsp sesame oil

In a small jug, combine the honey, sauces, sherry and cornflour.

Heat the wok, add the groundnut oil and, when the oil is very hot and begins to smoke, add the garlic and ginger, stirring for ½ minute. Add the pork and stir for 3 minutes. Add the cornflour mixture and stir for 2 minutes. Add the spring onions and stir for 1 minute. Add half the sesame seeds and stir for ½ minute. Add the sesame oil and stir for 1 minute. Remove the wok from the heat and sprinkle with the remaining sesame seeds before serving.

VEAL AND LIME CURRY

This is a mildly hot curry which looks as delicious as it tastes. Serve it with white rice and finely sliced red chilli. Serves 4.

15ml/1 tbsp groundnut oil
2-3 tbsp red curry paste
450g/1lb veal, cut into 2.5x2.5cm/1x1in pieces
400g/14oz baby sweetcorn, cut into halves
400ml/14fl oz coconut milk

2 tbsp lime rind
2 dried lime leaves
1 green chilli, deseeded and cut into rings
15ml/1 tbsp fish sauce
1 red chilli, deseeded and cut into thin rings

Heat the wok, add the groundnut oil and, when the oil is very hot and begins to smoke, mix in the curry paste. Stir for 1/2 minute. Add the veal and stir for 3-4 minutes or until cooked. Add the sweetcorn, coconut milk, lime rind, lime leaves, green chilli and fish sauce. Stir for 3-4 minutes or until the liquid has reduced by a quarter. Sprinkle with the red chilli rings.

MEXICAN STIR-FRY BEEF

This is a mildly spicy recipe from Mexico and is always a great favourite with the whole family. Serves 4.

15ml/1 tbsp groundnut oil
2 onions, finely chopped
2 garlic cloves, crushed
450g/1lb beef mince
200ml/7fl oz taco seasoning mix

450g/1lb tinned tomatoes
600g/1lb 7oz tinned kidney beans
1 tbsp whole cumin, crushed
30ml/2 tbsp hot taco sauce
1 red chilli, deseeded and very finely sliced

Heat the wok, add the groundnut oil and, when the oil is very hot and begins to smoke, add the onions and garlic and stir for 2 minutes or until the onions are opaque. Add the beef and stir for 6-8 minutes. Add the taco seasoning mix, tomatoes, kidney beans, cumin and hot taco sauce. Stir for 5 minutes. Add the chilli and stir for 1 minute.

PORK, BROCCOLI AND OYSTER SAUCE

This recipe has a wonderfully subtle flavour and is very quick and easy to prepare. It is best served with plain white rice. Serves 4.

450g/1lb pork fillet, cut into bite-size pieces
30-45ml/2-3 tbsp oyster sauce
30ml/2 tbsp groundnut oil

12 baby sweetcorn, cut diagonally into 2.5cm/1in lengths
200g/7oz broccoli, cut into small florets
1 chilli, deseeded and finely sliced (optional)

Marinate the pork in the oyster sauce.

Heat the wok, add the groundnut oil and, when the oil is very hot, add the sweetcorn, broccoli and chilli (if using). Stir for 2-3 minutes. Add the pork and sauce and stir for 4-5 minutes or until the pork is cooked and the vegetables are tender but still crisp.

WARM CHICKEN SALAD

This is a delicious summer lunch dish or can be served a starter. Serves 4.

3 chicken breasts, skinned
2 tbsp mustard
Juice of ½ lemon
1 tsp cornflour
2 slices bread
1 garlic clove
30ml/2 tbsp olive oil
15ml/1 tbsp groundnut oil

1 cos lettuce, leaves separated
25 cherry tomatoes
1 ripe avocado, diced
Salt
Freshly ground black pepper
Parmesan cheese shavings
Fresh parsley leaves to garnish

Cut the chicken into 1cm/½in wide strips. Marinate it in a bowl with the mustard, lemon juice and cornflour for 15 minutes. To make the croûtons, toast the bread lightly. Rub the toast with the garlic clove and cut it into small cubes. Heat the wok, add the olive oil and, when the oil is very hot, add the toast cubes and stir for 1 minute until golden. Remove them from the wok and drain on kitchen paper. Wipe out the wok then reheat, add the groundnut oil and, when oil is very hot and begins to smoke, add the chicken along with the marinade. Stir for 5 minutes. Add the lettuce, tomatoes and avocado. Stir for 1 minute. Season with salt and freshly ground black pepper. Place the contents of the wok into a large serving dish. Garnish with the croûtons, Parmesan shavings and parsley.

Above: Warm Chicken Salad

VEAL, AUBERGINE AND TOMATOES

This very colourful layered dish looks and tastes its best when served with a mixed green salad and white rice. Serves 4.

2 medium-sized aubergines	1 tbsp orange and mandarin rind, chopped
Salt	15ml/1 tbsp balsamic vinegar
75ml/5 tbsp groundnut oil	Freshly ground black pepper
3 garlic cloves, crushed	450g/1lb veal, cut into 5cm/2in cubes
2 medium-sized onions, sliced into rings	2 tbsp fresh basil, chopped
900g/2lb tinned plum tomatoes	

Slice the aubergines into 5mm/¼ in thick rounds. Lay these on kitchen paper, sprinkle with salt and leave for 10 minutes. Pat the aubergines dry with another sheet of kitchen paper, and then divide into three portions, for cooking in batches.

Heat the wok, add about 30-45ml/2-3 tbsp groundnut oil and, when the oil is very hot and begins to smoke, add half of the crushed garlic. Stir for ½ minute. Remove the garlic from the wok and discard it. Lay some of the aubergine slices flat in the wok, moving them around until golden brown on one side. Turn them to cook the other side. Now remove the aubergines and drain them on kitchen paper. Repeat this process until all the aubergine is cooked, removing the cooked slices from the wok as you proceed and placing them in a warm dish. Keep them hot, though!

Wipe out the wok with kitchen paper and reheat, adding 15ml/1 tbsp groundnut oil. When the oil is very hot and begins to smoke, add the onion rings and stir these for 2-3 minutes or until the onion is opaque. Add the tomatoes, orange and mandarin rind, vinegar, and a seasoning of pepper and stir until heated through. Remove everything from the wok and layer on top of the aubergine. Again, keep the dish hot.

Wipe out the wok as before and then reheat it. Add another 15ml/1 tbsp groundnut oil and, when the oil is very hot and begins to smoke, add the veal and the rest of the garlic and stir for 3-4 minutes or until cooked. Stir through the basil and season it with salt and pepper. Remove from the wok and layer the veal on top of the aubergine and tomatoes.

STIR-FRIED QUAIL WITH QUAIL EGGS AND OYSTER MUSHROOMS

This is an interesting blend of 'East meets West'. Serve with brown rice to make the most of the garlic butter and a green salad. Serves 4.

8 quail	3 garlic cloves, crushed
1 tbsp honey	200g/7oz oyster mushrooms
30ml/2 tbsp hot water	6 tbsp fresh parsley, finely chopped
12 quail eggs	Salt
15ml/1 tbsp groundnut oil	Freshly ground black pepper
50g/2oz butter	

With a heavy knife, cut out the backbone of each quail. Open up the quail and flatten it. Clean both inside and out. In a small jug, mix the honey and water and brush this over the quail.

Boil the quail eggs for 3 minutes, drain immediately and allow to cool before peeling off the shells. Rinse well.

Heat the wok, add the groundnut oil and, when the oil is very hot and begins to smoke, add as many of the quail as possible, laying them skin side up. Place the lid on the wok and leave to cook for 6-7 minutes. Turn the quail and leave them, again with the lid on, for 2-3 minutes to brown the skin. (To check that the quail is cooked, prick the thickest part of the thigh and if only clear liquid runs out, the quail are done.) Remove the quail from the wok and place in a warm oven while the remaining quail is being cooked.

Remove the wok from the heat and remove any excess oil. Reheat the wok and add the butter and garlic and stir for ½ minute. Add the mushrooms, the hard-boiled quail eggs and parsley, and stir for 3-4 minutes. Now layer this over the quail. Pour over the remaining garlic butter and season with salt and pepper to taste.

TURKEY, REDCURRANT JELLY AND MINT

This has a wonderful light fresh flavour. It makes a terrific luncheon dish when served with a mixed green salad or a main meal served with sliced boiled potatoes. Serves 4.

3 tbsp redcurrant jelly	15ml/1 tbsp groundnut oil
½ tsp cornflour	10 sprigs mint, chopped
450g/1lb turkey breast, sliced into strips	

In a large bowl, mix together the redcurrant jelly and cornflour. Add the turkey strips and marinate for 5 minutes.

Heat the wok, add the groundnut oil and, when the oil is very hot and begins to smoke, add the turkey along with the marinade. Stir for 3-5 minutes until the meat is well browned. Add the mint and stir for 2 minutes.

Right: Veal, Aubergine and Tomatoes

LEMON CHICKEN AND SWEET PEPPERS

The combination of lemon and mint gives a distinctive and fresh taste. Serve in roasted pepper shells with rice or sliced boiled potatoes and a fresh green salad. Serves 4.

450g/1lb chicken breast, cut into bite-size pieces
Juice of 1 lemon
Grated rind of 1 lemon
Freshly ground black pepper
15ml/1 tbsp groundnut oil
50g/2oz red pepper, deseeded and cut into long strips

50g/2oz green pepper, deseeded and cut into long strips
50g/2oz orange or yellow pepper, deseeded and cut into long strips
3 tbsp fresh mint, finely chopped

In a large bowl, combine the chicken, lemon juice, rind and black pepper.

Heat the wok, add the groundnut oil and, when the oil is very hot and begins to smoke, add the strips of pepper and stir for 1 minute. Carefully add the chicken and stir for 4-5 minutes. Add the mint and stir for 1 minute or until the chicken is cooked.

PINEAPPLE BEEF

Probably the first time you've thought of these two ingredients together but you won't be disappointed when you try this dish. Best served with rice or noodles. Serves 4.

450g/1lb beef fillet, cut into 6cm/2½in strips
15ml/1 tbsp groundnut oil
1 garlic clove, finely chopped
1 tsp fresh ginger, thinly sliced
2 spring onions, finely sliced diagonally
1 red pepper, deseeded and diced
1 red chilli, deseeded and cut into thin rings
4 pineapple slices, cut into triangular chunks (tinned will do)

FOR THE MARINADE
1 tsp cornflour
30ml/2 tbsp pale dry sherry
10 turns of freshly ground black pepper
1 tsp salt

30ml/2 tbsp light soy sauce
15ml/1 tbsp water
30ml/2 tbsp sesame oil

In a large bowl, combine all the ingredients for the marinade. Soak the beef in the marinade for 15-20 minutes.

Heat the wok, add the groundnut oil and, when the oil is very hot and begins to smoke, add the garlic, ginger and spring onions. Stir for 1 minute. Add the beef along with the marinade, red pepper and chilli and stir for 3-4 minutes. Then add the pineapple and stir for 2 minutes or until the pineapple is hot.

REDCURRANT JELLY LAMB

The classic combination of mint and lamb in this dish has the added interest of the redcurrant jelly. Great when served with wild rice. Serves 4.

4 tbsp redcurrant jelly
4 tbsp mint, finely chopped
450g/1lb lamb fillet, sliced across the grain into 1cm/½in thick rounds

15ml/1 tbsp groundnut oil
200g/7oz runner beans, trimmed and cut into 4cm/1½in lengths

Combine the redcurrant jelly with the mint and leave the lamb to marinate in this for 15 minutes.

Heat the wok, add the groundnut oil and, when the oil is hot and begins to smoke, add the lamb along with the marinade and stir for 2-3 minutes or until the lamb is browned on both sides. Finally, add the beans and stir for 2-3 minutes until beans are cooked but still crisp.

TURKEY WITH WATER CHESTNUTS AND CHOI SUM

The crunchy texture of the water chestnuts complements the choi sum beautifully. Serve on its own or with noodles. Serves 4.

450g/1lb turkey breast, sliced into strips
15ml/1 tbsp groundnut oil
15ml/1 tbsp sesame oil
10 water chestnuts, rinsed and drained, and cut into 3mm/⅛in thick slices

150g/5oz choi sum, stalks removed and leaves separated
Salt
Freshly ground black pepper

FOR THE MARINADE
½ tsp salt
15ml/1 tbsp light soy sauce
1 tsp pale dry sherry

3 turns of freshly ground black pepper
½ tsp cornflour
10ml/2 tsp water

In a large bowl, mix together the marinade ingredients and marinate the turkey for 15 minutes.

Heat the wok, add the groundnut and sesame oils. When the oils are very hot, add the turkey along with the marinade. Stir for 2 minutes. Add the water chestnuts and stir for 1 minute. Add the choi sum and stir for 2 minutes until the leaves begin to wilt. Season with salt and pepper to taste.

Right: Lemon Chicken and Sweet Peppers

SPICY PORK WITH APPLES

Pork and apples are a classic combination and they are greatly enhanced in this dish by the addition of cloves and cinnamon. Delicious served with stir-fried red cabbage. Serves 4.

200ml/7fl oz white wine vinegar
165g/5½oz soft brown sugar
4 whole cloves
1 cinnamon stick, 4cm/1½in long
550g/1¼lb dessert apples, peeled, cored and cut into eighths

75g/3oz raisins (optional)
450g/1lb pork fillet, cut into 5mm/¼in thick slices

In a small jug, combine the vinegar and brown sugar.

Heat the wok to a low temperature. Add the vinegar and sugar and stir until the sugar is dissolved. Add the cloves and cinnamon stick and bring to simmering point, stirring for ½ minute. Remove the cloves and cinnamon. Then add the apples and raisins (if using) and stir carefully until the apples are tender but still firm. When they are ready, pour off the syrup into a warm jug, leaving the apples in the wok. Add the pork slices and toss for about 4 minutes or until the pork is cooked. Finally pour the syrup over the pork and stir well.

CHICKEN AND ALMONDS

This combination has a hint of the Orient and is a great starter for more exotic flavours which may be served later. It's best served with white rice. Serves 4.

15ml/1 tbsp light soy sauce
30ml/2 tbsp pale dry sherry
2 tsp cornflour
30ml/2 tbsp groundnut oil
450g/1lb chicken breasts, sliced into strips
2 garlic cloves, crushed or finely chopped
1 tsp fresh ginger, finely chopped

3 spring onions, sliced diagonally
½ red pepper, deseeded and cut into strips
½ green pepper, deseeded and cut into strips
75g/3oz almonds, sliced and roasted
2 tsp sesame oil

In a small jug, mix together the soy sauce, sherry and cornflour. Heat the wok, add the groundnut oil and, when the oil is very hot and begins to smoke, add the chicken strips and stir for 3 minutes or until the chicken turns white. Carefully remove with a slotted spoon and set aside in a warm place. Add the garlic and ginger to the wok and stir for ½ minute. Now add the spring onions and the peppers and stir for 1 minute. Remove the wok from the heat and pour in the soy sauce mixture. Return to the heat and stir for 1 minute. Add the chicken and the almonds and stir for another 2 minutes. Finally, add the sesame oil and stir for 1 minute.

CITRUS LAMB AND VEGETABLES

The combination of flavours in this recipe is delicious with just a hint of citrus to add extra piquancy. It's best served with white rice. Serves 4.

450g/1lb lean lamb fillet, sliced into strips
1 tsp citrus or lemon pepper
15ml/1 tbsp pale dry sherry
15ml/1 tbsp fish sauce
15ml/1 tbsp oyster sauce
2 tsp cornflour
15ml/1 tbsp groundnut oil
2 garlic cloves, finely chopped
2 tsp fresh ginger, grated
150g/5oz carrots, cut into 2cm/1in julienne strips

150g/5oz mangetout, topped and cut into 2cm/1in lengths
½ red pepper, deseeded and cut into 2cm/1in long strips
½ green pepper, deseeded and cut into 2cm/1in long strips
3 spring onions, finely chopped diagonally
1 tsp lemon myrtle oil

Toss the lamb in the citrus or lemon pepper. In a small jug, combine the sherry, sauces and cornflour, and mix well.

Heat the wok, add the groundnut oil and, when the oil is very hot and begins to smoke, add the garlic and ginger. Stir for ½ minute. Add the lamb and stir for 3-4 minutes until the meat is well browned. With a slotted spoon, remove the meat and set aside in a warm place.

Reheat the wok and add the carrots, mangetout and peppers. Stir for 3 minutes. Add the cornflour mixture and stir for 2 minutes. Return the lamb and stir for a further 3 minutes. Add the spring onions and stir for 1 minute. Finally, add the lemon myrtle oil, stir for 1/2 minute.

LAMB, APRICOT AND CORIANDER

The sweetness of the apricots and the distinctive taste of the coriander blend perfectly to create this wonderful dish. Serves 4.

15ml/1 tbsp pale dry sherry
1 tsp cornflour
15ml/1 tbsp groundnut oil
450g/1 lb lamb fillet, sliced

1 onion, finely sliced
1 garlic clove, crushed or finely chopped
250g/9 oz tinned apricots in natural juice
1 tbsp coriander, finely chopped

In a small jug combine the sherry and cornflour. Set aside.

Heat the wok, add the groundnut oil and, when the oil is very hot and begins to smoke, add the lamb and stir for 3 minutes or until all the meat is browned and tender. With a slotted spoon, carefully remove the lamb and set aside in a warm place.

Return the wok to the heat and add the onion and garlic. Stir for 2 minutes. Add the apricots and the juice and stir for 3 minutes. Pour over the cornflour mixture and stir for 2 minutes. Add the lamb and stir for 1 minute. Finally, add the coriander and stir for 1 minute.

Right: Spicy Pork with Apples

Above: Chicken and Vegetables

CHICKEN AND VEGETABLES

The easiest way of coating the poultry for this recipe is by placing it in a plastic bag along with the cornflour. This terrific family favourite, when accompanied by brown rice or noodles, will serve 6.

250g/9oz + 2 tbsp cornflour
350ml/12fl oz water
2 chicken stock cubes
2 whole chicken breasts, skinned
4 chicken thigh fillets., skinned
2 egg whites
75ml/5 tbsp groundnut oil
1 garlic clove, finely chopped
½ tbsp fresh ginger, finely chopped
1 onion, finely sliced
6 spring onions, cut into 1cm/½in lengths

¼ tsp Chinese five spice
2 carrots, medium to finely sliced
100g/4oz broccoli, cut into florets
75g/3oz mangetout, sliced
150g/5oz baby patty pan sqaush, quartered
2 celery sticks, sliced diagonally
1 red pepper, deseeded and sliced
150g/5oz mixed mushrooms, sliced
30ml/2 tbsp light soy sauce
10ml/2 tsp Worcestershire sauce

In a jug, mix together 2 tbsp cornflour, the water and the chicken stock cubes. Set aside.

Slice all of the chicken into strips 1cm/½in thick.

Place the egg whites into a bowl and beat lightly with a fork until they bubble. Toss the chicken strips in 120g/4½oz cornflour and then dip the chicken into the egg whites. (You will have to do this in several batches.)

Heat the wok, add 45ml/3 tbsp groundnut oil and, when the oil is very hot and begins to smoke, add the chicken and stir in batches until the chicken is tender. Drain well and set aside in a warm place. Add the remaining groundnut oil to the wok and, when hot, add the garlic, ginger and onions. Stir for 1 minute. Add the Chinese five spice and stir for ½ minute. Add the carrots, broccoli, mangetout, patty pan squash, celery, red pepper and mushrooms, in that order, and stir for 3 minutes until the vegetables are tender but still crisp. Add the soy sauce and Worcestershire sauce and stir through. Remove the wok from the heat and stir in the cornflour mixture, then return to the heat and stir for 2 minutes. Return the chicken to the wok and stir for 1 minute. Serve immediately as the vegetables tend to lose their crispness if they are left to stand.

LAMB KIDNEYS, BACON AND GARLIC

This is a spoil-yourself breakfast treat or a terrific light lunch served either with a crisp green salad or on a simple bed of white rice. Serves 4.

450g/1lb lamb kidneys
2 tsp Worcestershire sauce
2 tsp cornflour
15ml/1 tbsp pale dry sherry
15ml/1 tbsp water

1 tsp brown sugar
15ml/1 tbsp groundnut oil
2 garlic cloves, crushed
3 rashers bacon, cut into strips, rind removed

To prepare the kidneys, first remove the outer skin and flatten them. Remove the knob of fat from the centre and slice the kidneys thickly. Plunge them into boiling water for a few minutes. Drain and repeat this process again to remove any bitter taste. Pat the kidneys dry with kitchen paper.

In a small jug, combine the Worcestershire sauce, cornflour, sherry, water and sugar.

Heat the wok, add the groundnut oil and, when the oil is very hot and begins to smoke, add the crushed garlic and stir for ½ minute. Add the bacon and stir for 2 minutes. Add the kidneys and stir for 1 minute. Add the cornflour mixture and stir for 2-3 minutes or until the kidneys are tender.

PORK AND BLACK OLIVES

This colourful dish tastes as good as it looks. But remember that soy sauce is salty, so always taste before adding salt. Serves 4.

15ml/1 tbsp pale dry sherry
15ml/1 tbsp light soy sauce
1 tsp cornflour
15ml/1 tbsp groundnut oil
450g/1lb lean pork, cut into bite-size pieces
100g/4oz small mangetout, trimmed

1 medium-sized red pepper, deseeded and diced
10-12 black olives, pitted
1 tsp sesame oil
Salt
Freshly ground black pepper

In a small jug combine the sherry, soy sauce and cornflour. Set aside.

Heat the wok, add the groundnut oil and, when the oil is very hot and begins to smoke, add the pork. Stir for 2-3 minutes. Add the mangetout and the red pepper, stirring for 2 minutes. Now pour on the cornflour mixture and stir for 1 minute. Add the olives and stir for 1-2 minutes or until the vegetables are cooked but still crisp. Finally, add the sesame oil and stir for ½ minute. Season to taste.

GARLIC QUAIL AND VEGETABLES

This looks and tastes fantastic and, when served on a white plate, is good enough for any dinner party. The contrasting textures of the chewy mushrooms and the crisp water chestnuts are delicious. Serves 4.

4 quail (allow 1 per person)
Salt
Freshly ground black pepper
30ml/2 tbsp oyster sauce
15ml/1 tbsp light soy sauce
15ml/1 tbsp pale dry sherry
15ml/1 tbsp water
2 tsp cornflour
15ml/1 tbsp groundnut oil
1 garlic clove, crushed

6 dried shiitake mushrooms, soaked for 20 minutes, squeezed and sliced, and hard stems removed
50g/2oz mixed red and green peppers, deseeded and sliced into 2.5cm/1in lengths
50g/2oz mangetout, trimmed and cut diagonally into 2.5cm/1in lengths
100g/4oz tinned water chestnuts, rinsed in cold water and sliced

Clean the quail well and pat dry. Chop each one into 4-6 pieces. (A Chinese cleaver is ideal for this procedure.) Place the quail in a large bowl and season with salt and freshly ground black pepper.

In a small jug, combine the sauces, sherry, water and cornflour. Mix well.

Heat the wok, add the groundnut oil and, when the oil is very hot and begins to smoke, add the garlic and stir for ½ minute. Add the quail pieces and stir for 4-5 minutes until well browned. With a slotted spoon, remove them and set aside in a warm place. (You may have to do this in two batches, depending on the size of your wok.) Reheat the wok and add the mushrooms, peppers, mangetout and water chestnuts. Stir for 2-3 minutes. Add the cornflour mixture and stir for 2 minutes. Add the quail pieces and stir for a further 2-3 minutes.

RED CHICKEN CURRY

This is mildly hot and tastes at its best when served with plain white rice. Serves 4.

450g/1lb chicken breasts, cut into bite-size pieces
65g/2 ½oz plain flour
45ml/3 tbsp groundnut oil
1-2 tbsp red curry paste
400ml/14fl oz coconut milk

1 generous tbsp crunchy peanut butter
15ml/1 tbsp fish sauce
1 red chilli, deseeded and finely chopped
Salt
Freshly ground black pepper
Fresh coconut shavings to garnish (optional)

Coat the chicken pieces with the flour, shaking off any excess.

Heat the wok, add the groundnut oil and, when the oil is very hot and begins to smoke, add the chicken pieces and stir for 3-4 minutes or until browned. With a slotted spoon, remove the chicken and set aside in a warm place. Pour away any remaining oil and wipe the wok clean. Reheat the wok and add the curry paste. Mash for ½ minute. Add the coconut milk and peanut butter and mix well. Stir until the mixture starts to simmer. Add the fish sauce and the chilli. Stir for 2-3 minutes. Add the chicken pieces and simmer until the chicken is hot. Season to taste and sprinkle with the coconut shavings if using.

Above: Red Chicken Curry

27

BEEF, OLIVES AND MUSHROOMS

Stoned sliced olives are easier to eat, but whole olives make for a spectacular presentation. Cooking time of the meat depends on how rare you prefer your steak. Allow 2 slices of beef per person. Serves 4.

30ml/2 tbsp oyster sauce	450g/1lb fillet steak (rump or sirloin),
15ml/1 tbsp dark soy sauce	cut into 1cm/½in thick slices, seasoned
15ml/1 tbsp pale dry sherry	with freshly ground pepper
15ml/1 tbsp water	100g/4oz broccoli, cut into small florets
2 tsp cornflour	100g/4oz button mushrooms, sliced
15ml/1 tbsp groundnut oil	12-18 assorted olives

In a small jug, combine the sauces, sherry, water and cornflour. Set aside.

Heat the wok, add the groundnut oil and, when the oil is very hot and begins to smoke, add the meat and stir for 2 minutes or it is browned. Remove the beef from the wok with a slotted spoon and set it aside in a warm place. Add the broccoli to the wok and stir for 2 minutes. Toss in the mushrooms and stir for 2 minutes. Now add the cornflour mixture and stir everything for 1 minute. Finally, add the olives and meat slices and stir for 1-2 minutes until the meat is hot.

MEXICAN-STYLE CHICKEN WINGS

This is a great family recipe – children love it because it's not too hot. Adjust the taco seasoning according to the degree of 'heat' your family can cope with. Serves 4.

90-120ml/6-8 tbsp taco seasoning mix	850g/1lb 14oz tinned kidney beans
120ml/8 tbsp groundnut oil	450g/1lb tinned tomatoes
650g/1lb 9oz chicken wings	1 green chilli, cut into thin rings
15ml/1 tbsp olive oil	30ml/2 tbsp hot taco sauce (optional)
2 onions, roughly chopped	1 tbsp whole cumin, crushed

Mix the taco seasoning with 90ml/6 tbsp groundnut oil and coat the chicken with it. Leave to marinate for 15 minutes. (The longer it is left the hotter it becomes.)

Heat the wok, add the remaining groundnut oil and, when the oil is very hot and begins to smoke, add the chicken without the marinade. Stir for 6-8 minutes. Prick the thickest part of each chicken piece to check if it is cooked. Remove the chicken from the wok and set aside on a warm plate. Wipe out the wok.

Reheat the wok to a medium heat and add the olive oil and onions. Stir for 2 minutes or until the onions are opaque. Add the kidney beans, tomatoes, chilli, hot taco sauce (if using) and cumin. Stir for 3-4 minutes. Remove everything from the wok and place in a warm dish with the chicken wings on top.

LAMB WITH PLUM SAUCE

The piquant flavour of the sauce adds an extra taste to the lamb. It's best served with rice. Serves 4.

30ml/2 tbsp plum sauce	1 garlic clove, crushed
15ml/1 tbsp pale dry sherry	450g/1lb lean lamb fillet, cut into
15ml/1 tbsp water	1cm/½in thick rounds
1 tsp cornflour	100g/4oz sugarsnap peas
15ml/1 tbsp groundnut oil	100g/4oz button mushrooms, sliced

In a small jug, combine the plum sauce, sherry, water and cornflour. Mix well.

Heat the wok, add the groundnut oil, and when the oil is very hot and begins to smoke, add the garlic and stir for ½ minute. Add the lamb and stir for 3 minutes until browned. With a slotted spoon, remove the lamb from the wok and set aside in a warm place. Reheat the wok and add the peas and mushrooms. Stir for 2-3 minutes. Add the cornflour mixture and stir for 1 minute. Add the lamb and stir for 2-3 minutes until the vegetables are cooked but still crisp.

LEMON VEAL

The tang of lemon adds a wonderful flavour to the veal and the addition of myrtle oil makes it even more delicious. Serves 4.

2 tsp lemon juice	100g/4oz green beans, sliced diagonally
Grated rind of ½ lemon	into 2.5cm/1in lengths
2 tsp brown sugar	100g/4oz button mushroom, thinly sliced
15ml/1 tbsp pale dry sherry	3 spring onions, sliced
1 tsp cornflour	1 tsp lemon myrtle oil (optional)
15ml/1 tbsp groundnut oil	Citrus or lemon pepper
450g/1lb veal, thinly sliced	

In a small jug, combine the lemon juice and rind, sugar, sherry and cornflour.

Heat the wok, add the groundnut oil and, when the oil is very hot and begins to smoke, add the veal and stir for 2-3 minutes until browned and tender. Add the beans and stir for 1 minute, add the mushrooms and stir for 2 minutes. Add the cornflour mixture and stir for 2 minutes. Add the spring onions and stir for 2 minutes until the vegetables are cooked but still crisp. Stir through the lemon myrtle oil (if using) and finish with citrus or lemon pepper to taste.

Right: Beef, Olives and Mushrooms

CHICKEN, MUSHROOMS AND BASIL

You can use either sherry or vermouth in this dish – try both variations to decide which flavour you prefer. This is best served with Chinese egg noodles. Serves 4.

30ml/2 tbsp groundnut oil	100g/4oz baby corn, sliced on the diagonal
450g/1lb chicken breast, sliced into strips	30ml/2 tbsp pale dry sherry or white
2 leeks, finely sliced	vermouth
150g/5oz mixed mushrooms	45ml/3 tbsp lemon juice
½ red pepper, deseeded and sliced	1 tbsp fresh parsley, chopped
½ yellow pepper, deseeded and sliced	25g/1oz fresh basil, chopped
8 cherry tomatoes	

Heat the wok, add the groundnut oil and, when the oil is very hot and begins to smoke, add the chicken and stir for 3 minutes or until the chicken turns white. With a slotted spoon, remove the chicken from the wok and set aside in a warm place.

Add the leeks, mushrooms, peppers, tomatoes and corn to the wok and stir for 2-3 minutes until the vegetables are tender but still crisp. Add the sherry (or vermouth), lemon juice and herbs and stir for about 30 seconds. Return the chicken to the wok and stir through for 1 minute until it's very hot.

CITRUS PORK AND VEGETABLES

The slight tang of orange in this perfectly complements the pork. A great lunch dish that's best served with Brown Ginger Rice (see page 48). Serves 4.

30ml/2 tbsp freshly squeezed orange juice	1 garlic clove, crushed
Grated rind of ½ orange	1 tsp fresh ginger, grated
15ml/1 tbsp pale dry sherry	450g/1lb lean pork, cut into strips
2 tsp light soy sauce	100g/4oz button mushrooms, sliced
1 tsp cornflour	100g/4oz French beans, sliced diagonally
1 tsp brown sugar	in 3cm/1¼in lengths
15ml/1 tbsp groundnut oil	

In a small jug, combine the orange juice, rind, sherry, soy sauce, cornflour and brown sugar.

Heat the wok, add the groundnut oil and, when the oil is very hot and begins to smoke, add the garlic and ginger. Stir for ½ minute. Add the pork and stir for 3 minutes until the pork is browned. Add the mushrooms and beans and stir for 2 minutes. Add the cornflour mixture and stir for 3 minutes or until the vegetables are cooked but still crisp.

GARLIC CREAM CHICKEN WITH OYSTER MUSHROOMS

This is a super creamy garlic tasting dish and is best served with noodles or sliced boiled potatoes.

500g/1 lb chicken breast fillets,	75–100ml/3–4 fl oz single cream
cut into bite size pieces	4 tbsp chopped parsley
15ml/1 tbsp groundnut oil	Salt and freshly ground black pepper
200g/7 oz oyster mushrooms, sliced	to taste
100g/4 oz garlic-herb cheese, such as Boursin	

Heat the wok or large pan, add the groundnut oil and when oil is very hot and begins to smoke, add the chicken. Stir for 4 minutes or until the chicken turns white. Add the mushrooms and cheese and stir for 1 minute. Add the cream and stir for 2 minutes, adding a little more cream according to taste. Stir in the parsley and season to taste.

DUCK AND OLIVES

The combination of duck and olives may be unusual but it is guaranteed to be a delectable combination. Best accompanied by a green salad. Serves 4.

250g/9oz Chinese egg noodles	400g/14oz duck breast, cut into
1 tsp pale dry sherry	5mm/¼in thick slices
½ tsp cornflour	15ml/1 tbsp groundnut oil
2 sprigs thyme	25 mixed olives, pitted
2 sprigs rosemary	30ml/2 tbsp brandy
1 garlic clove, crushed	250ml/8fl oz chicken stock

Cook the noodles as directed on the packet. Drain them and set aside in a warm place.

In a large bowl, combine the sherry, cornflour, thyme, rosemary and garlic and mix well. Marinate the duck in this for 15 minutes. Heat the wok, add the groundnut oil and, when the oil is very hot and begins to smoke, add the duck, along with the marinade, and the olives. Stir for 1 minute. Add the brandy and ignite. When the flame burns off, stir for 2-3 minutes. Add the chicken stock and noodles. Stir for 1 minute. Remove the rosemary and season to taste. Bring to the boil and allow the liquid to reduce slightly before serving.

Right: Chicken, Mushrooms and Basil

Beef and Black Bean Sauce

This is a wonderfully aromatic dish thanks to the Chinese five spice seasoning. Serves 4.

15ml/1 tbsp dark soy sauce	*1 tsp Chinese five spice*
15ml/1 tbsp black bean sauce	*100g/4oz aspargus spears, sliced*
2 tsp cornflour	*150g/5oz mangetout, sliced*
15ml/1 tbsp water	*1 yellow pepper, deseeded and sliced*
30ml/2 tbsp groundnut oil	*1 red pepper, deseeded and sliced*
450g/1lb rump or sirloin steak, cut into	*Chopped fresh chilli (optional)*
thin strips	

In a jug, combine the sauces, cornflour and water. Heat the wok, add the groundnut oil and, when the oil is very hot and begins to smoke, add the meat and stir for 3-4 minutes. Add the five spice and vegetables. Stir for 1 minute. Remove the wok from the heat and stir in the cornflour mixture. Finally, return the wok to the heat and stir for 1 minute or until the vegetables are tender but still crisp.

Veal, Tomatoes, Leeks and Basil

Tomatoes and basil are always a perfect combination. Serve this dish for lunch accompanied by a green salad, or for supper accompanied by brown rice. Serves 4.

15ml/1 tbsp dry white vermouth	*250g/9oz tomatoes, skinned, deseeded*
1 tsp cornflour	*and chopped*
15ml/1 tbsp groundnut oil	*2 tbsp basil, chopped*
1 garlic clove, finely chopped	*15ml/1 tbsp basil oil*
450g/1lb veal, thinly sliced	*Salt*
2 small leeks, finely sliced diagonally	*Freshly ground black pepper*

In a small jug, combine the vermouth and cornflour. Mix well.

Heat the wok, add the groundnut oil and, when the oil is hot and begins to smoke, add the garlic and stir for ½ minute. Add the veal and stir for 2-3 minutes until the veal is browned. Add the leeks and tomatoes and stir for 2 minutes. Add the cornflour mixture and stir for 1 minute. Add the basil and stir for 1 minute. Stir through the basil oil and season with salt and pepper to taste.

Chicken, Water Chestnuts, Asparagus and Black Bean Sauce

This is a great combination of flavours and the crunchy texture of the water chestnuts adds extra interest. This is best served with white rice. Serves 4.

450g/1lb chicken breast, cut into	*10 tinned water chestnuts, rinsed well in*
bite-size pieces	*cold water and cut in half*
45ml/3 tbsp black bean sauce	*12 asparagus spears, cut into*
15ml/1 tbsp groundnut oil	*4cm/1½in lengths*
1 red chilli, very finely sliced (optional)	

Marinate the chicken in the black bean sauce for 15 minutes. Heat the wok, add the groundnut oil and, when the oil is very hot and begins to smoke, add the chilli if you are using it and stir for ½ minute. Add the chicken along with the marinade. Stir for 1 minute. Add the water chestnuts and the asparagus and stir for 4-5 minutes or until the vegetables are cooked but still crisp.

Citrus Beef

This is a delicious combination of sharp and sweet flavours. Serve this to your family with rice or a green salad. Serves 4.

450g/1lb lean eye of fillet beef, cut into	*30ml/2 tbsp dark soy sauce*
1cm/½in thick rounds	*2 tsp cornflour*
1 tsp Chinese five spice	*30ml/2 tbsp groundnut oil*
15ml/1 tbsp orange juice	*1 tsp fresh ginger, grated*
Finely grated rind of 1 orange	*100g/4oz fresh asparagus tips*
2 tsp brown sugar	*2 tsp sesame oil*
15ml/1 tbsp pale dry sherry	

Season the beef with the Chinese five spice. In a jug, combine the orange juice, orange rind, brown sugar, sherry, soy sauce and cornflour. Mix well. Heat the wok, add the groundnut oil and, when the oil is very hot and begins to smoke, add the ginger and stir for ½ minute. Add the beef and stir for 3-4 minutes, making sure both sides are browned. Remove the beef from the wok and set aside in a warm place. Reheat the wok and add the cornflour mixture. Stir for 1 minute. Add the asparagus and stir for 2-3 minutes. Add the meat and stir for 2 minutes. Add the sesame oil and stir for 1 minute.

Right: Beef and Black Bean Sauce

TURKEY WITH CITRUS–CRANBERRY SAUCE

The unusual combination of citrus and cranberries complements the turkey perfectly. Serves 4.

1 tbsp citrus rind, grated or shredded
85ml/3fl oz orange juice
30ml/2 tbsp lemon juice
175g/6oz cranberry sauce
15ml/1 tbsp pale dry sherry
2 tsp cornflour

15ml/1 tbsp groundnut oil
450g/1lb turkey breasts, sliced
2 spring onions, sliced diagonally
200g/7oz courgettes, sliced diagonally
Freshly ground red peppercorns

In a small jug, combine the citrus rind, juices, cranberry sauce, sherry and cornflour. Mix well and set aside.

Heat the wok, add the groundnut oil and, when the oil is very hot and begins to smoke, add the turkey. Stir for 3-4 minutes or until the turkey is tender. With a slotted spoon, remove the turkey from the wok and set aside in a warm place.

Return the wok to the heat and add the spring onions and courgettes and stir for 2 minutes. Add the sauce mixture and stir for 1 minute. Return the turkey to the wok and stir for 2 minutes or until hot. Season with freshly ground red pepper.

DUCK IN PLUM SAUCE

This dish is best served with boiled white rice and a fresh green salad. The duck crackling is a delicious addition. Serves 4.

450g/1lb duck breast with skin,
thinly sliced
15ml/1 tbsp water
15ml/1 tbsp pale dry sherry
45ml/3 tbsp plum sauce

30ml/2 tbsp groundnut oil
2 garlic cloves, crushed or sliced
3–4 spring onions, sliced
15ml/1 tbsp soy sauce (optional)

Remove the skin fom the duck and slice thinly. Slice the meat and set aside. In a jug, combine the the water, sherry and plum sauce. Heat a wok or large pan and add 1 tbsp of the oil. When it is hot and begins to smoke, add the dusk skin and stir for 2–3 minutes until golden brown and crisp. Remove from the wok with a slotted spoon and drain on kitchen towels. Wipe the wok clean and reheat. Add the remaining oil and when hot, add the garlic and stir for 30 seconds, then add the duck meat and stir for 3-4 minutes until the meat is well browned. Pour in the plum sauce mixture and stir for 2 minutes. Add the spring onions and stir for 1 minute. Stir in the soy sauce if using. Remove from the heat and serve topped with the duck skin crackling.

PORK WITH ASPARAGUS AND BLACK BEAN SAUCE

This is at its best in summer when the asparagus is fresh and in season. It makes a wonderful lunch dish when served with brown rice. Serves 4.

15ml/1 tbsp groundnut oil
450g/1lb lean pork, cut into strips
60ml/4 tbsp black bean sauce
12 fresh asparagus stalks, cut into
3 cm/1¼ in pieces
½ red pepper, deseeded and cut into
long strips

½ yellow pepper, deseeded and cut into
long strips
Salt
Freshly ground black pepper

Heat the wok and add the groundnut oil. When the oil is very hot and begins to smoke, add the pork and black bean sauce, stirring for 2 minutes. Add the asparagus and peppers and stir for 3 minutes or until the vegetables are cooked but still crisp. Season to taste and serve.

Right: Turkey with Citrus-Cranberry Sauce

FISH & SHELLFISH

Stir-frying is ideal for fish and shellfish as the cooking time is so brief. As long as the pieces are small, they will cook in no time at all and seafood retains its delicate flavour well when cooked rapidly. Experiment with different types of fish and shellfish and always buy the freshest ingredients available.

FISH IN BLACK BEAN SAUCE

This is quite perfect when served with Lemon Thai Rice (see page 46). Serves 4.

450g/1lb plaice fillet or cod, cut into bite-size pieces, all bones removed
45-60ml/3-4 tbsp black bean sauce
15ml/1 tbsp groundnut oil
½ red or orange pepper, deseeded and cut into long strips
150g/5oz broccoli, cut into small florets
Salt
Freshly ground black pepper

FOR THE SAUCE
30ml/2 tbsp light soy sauce
50ml/2fl oz fish stock
1 small red chilli, deseeded and cut into thin slices
5 thin slices fresh ginger

Marinate the fish in the black bean sauce for 10 minutes. In a jug, combine the sauce ingredients and set aside.

Heat the wok, add the groundnut oil and, when the oil is very hot and begins to smoke, add the pepper and broccoli. Stir for 2 minutes. Add the sauce and stir everything for 2-3 minutes. With a slotted spoon, remove the pepper and broccoli and set this aside in a hot place. Lower the heat under the wok and add the fish pieces, without the black bean marinade. Stir carefully for 2-3 minutes, depending on the size of the fish. Season to taste and place on serving plates garnished with the hot vegetables. Heat any remaining pan juices with the black bean marinade until quite hot and pour this over the fish just before serving.

PRAWNS AND MANGO

What a delicious combination. This is a great starter or light lunch when served on its own, or add some rice and noodles to make a main meal. Serves 4.

12 large green prawns, peeled and deveined, tails left on
120ml/4fl oz mango pickle

15ml/2 tbsp groundnut oil
2 fresh mangoes, peeled and cut into large bite-size pieces

In a large bowl, marinate the prawns in the mango pickle for 5 minutes. Turn them a few times to ensure an even flavour.

Heat the wok, add the groundnut oil and, when the oil is very hot and begins to smoke, add the prawns along with the marinade and stir for 3 minutes. With a slotted spoon, remove any pieces of mango pickle. Now add the fresh mango pieces and stir for 1 minute or until the prawns are pink and the mango is hot.

SALT AND PEPPER SQUID

Perfect as a finger food for a party, this can also be served as a starter for 4.

FOR THE BATTER
100g/4oz self-raising flour
150ml/5fl oz water
½ tsp salt

450g/1lb squid tubes
60-90ml/4-6 tbsp groundnut oil – depending on the shape of your wok

2 tbsp salt
10 turns of freshly ground black pepper
1 red chilli, deseeded and finely chopped

Make the batter by mixing together the flour and salt, and then whisking in the water. Beat until smooth.

Clean the squid tubes, removing the head if necessary, and the backbone. Cut the squid into 1cm/¼in thick rings and dip them into the batter.

Heat the wok, add the groundnut oil and, when the oil is very hot and begins to smoke, add the squid. Stir for 1 minute. Finally add the salt, pepper and chilli and stir for 2 minutes. Serve with lemon wedges.

Above: Tuna and Guacamole Salad

PRAWNS, SCALLOPS, MANGETOUT AND GINGER

For best results, keep all the pieces of seafood and vegetables the same size. This looks more attractive and the ingredients cook more evenly. (See picture page 9.)

250g/9oz fresh scallops with coral
250g/9oz green prawns, peeled and deveined
15ml/1 tbsp pale dry sherry
15ml/1 tbsp light soy sauce
1 tsp cornflour
15ml/1 tbsp groundnut oil
15ml1 tbsp freshly grated ginger

1 garlic clove, crushed
1 spring onion, finely chopped
250g/9oz green prawns, peeled and deveined
200g/8oz mangetout, trimmed
1 red pepper, seeded and chopped
2 tsp sesame oil

Wash and dry the scallops. Mix the sherry, soy sauce and cornflour.

Heat the wok or large pan, add the groundnut oil and, when the oil is very hot and begins to smoke, add the ginger, garlic and spring onions. Stir for 30 seconds. Add the mangetout and red pepper and stir for 1 minute. Add the prawns and scallops and stir for 1 minute.

Remove the pan from the heat and carefully stir in the cornflour mixture. Return the pan to the heat and stir for 2 minutes or until the scallops are firm and the prawns turn pink. Stir in the sesame oil and stir for 1 minute.

TUNA AND GUACAMOLE SALAD

Tuna with guacamole is simply fabulous and accompanied by the dressing with coriander it has an extra tang. To make a good guacamole, it is important to taste-as-you-go and adjust accordingly. This is a quite delicious luncheon or light supper dish. Serves 4.

4 slices thick bread
30ml/2 tbsp olive oil
1 garlic clove
60ml/4 tbsp groundnut oil
450g/1lb fresh tuna, cut into 2.5x2.5cm/1x1in pieces
150g/5oz baby spinach (use whole leaves)
12 cherry tomatoes

FOR THE GUACAMOLE
1 large ripe avocado
1-2 garlic cloves, crushed
¼ tsp salt
Juice of 1 lemon

FOR THE DRESSING
60ml/4tbsp water
25ml/1½ tbsp light soy sauce
5 thin slices fresh ginger
1 red chilli, deseeded and finely sliced
Grated rind of 1 lemon
1 tbsp fresh coriander, finely chopped
1 tsp pale dry sherry
Salt
Freshly ground black pepper

In a jug, combine the dressing ingredients and let them stand for 15 minutes to ensure a full flavour. Toast the bread lightly. Brush it with olive oil and rub each piece with the garlic clove. Cut the toast into triangles.

Heat the wok, add the groundnut oil and, when the oil is very hot and begins to smoke, add the toast pieces and stir for 1-2 minutes until golden brown. Remove them and drain on kitchen paper. Wipe the wok clean.

For the guacamole, mash the avocado with the garlic and salt. Add the lemon juice and stir thoroughly.

Heat the wok, add the remaining olive oil and, when the oil is hot, add the tuna and stir for 1-2 minutes or until cooked. (The tuna should be pink in the centre, not cooked through entirely.) With a slotted spoon, remove the tuna and set it aside in a warm place. Add the baby spinach leaves and tomatoes and stir for 1 minute until the spinach starts to darken and go slightly limp. Remove the wok from the heat.

Arrange the salad ingredients on a plate, add the tuna, croûtons and guacamole. Serve with a side bowl of the dressing.

SMOKED FISH WITH VEGETABLES

The combination of smoked fish and vegetables is delicious and is best served with plain white rice or Lemon Thai Rice (see page 46). Serves 4.

400g/14oz smoked fish
15ml/1 tbsp light soy sauce
15ml/1 tbsp pale dry sherry
30ml/2 tbsp lemon juice
15ml/1 tbsp groundnut oil
150g/5oz broccoli, cut into small florets and stems

150g/5oz French or runner beans, cut into 4cm/1½in lengths diagonally
100g/4oz orange or red peppers, cut into 2.5x2.5cm/1x1in pieces diagonally
1 tbsp spring onions, cut diagonally
25g/1oz chives, finely chopped

Place the fish in a shallow pan of simmering water and poach for 5 minutes or until just cooked. Remove the fish from the pan and drain well. Carefully cut into pieces about 2.5x4cm/1x1½in. Set aside in a warm place.

While the fish is cooking, mix together the soy sauce, sherry and lemon juice in a small jug, and set aside.

Heat the wok, add the groundnut oil and, when the oil is very hot and begins to smoke, add the broccoli, beans and peppers. Stir for 1 minute. Add the spring onions and stir for 1 minute or until the vegetables are tender but still crisp. Add the sauce mixture and stir for 1 minute. Carefully add the fish pieces and half of the chives and stir for 1 minute, making sure not to break up the fish. Finally, serve with the remaining chives sprinkled on top.

COD AND PRAWNS IN LIME SAUCE

Give an extra tang to fish with this lime sauce. This makes a perfect starter for 6-8 or a main course, served with rice or noodles, for 4.

4 large green prawns, peeled, deveined and cut into large pieces
250g/9oz cod fillet, cut into bite-size pieces
Juice and grated rind of 2 limes
15ml/1 tbsp groundnut oil
1 garlic clove, crushed

2 tsp fresh ginger, grated
15ml/1 tbsp fish sauce
1 red chilli, deseeded and finely chopped
2 spring onions, cut lengthways into strips
2 tbsp fresh coriander, roughly chopped

Marinate the prawns and cod in the lime juice and rind for 30 minutes. Remove the prawns and fish and pat dry with kitchen paper, reserving the liquid.

Heat the wok, add the groundnut oil and, when the oil is very hot and begins to smoke, add the garlic and ginger and stir for ½ minute. Add the prawns and stir for 1-2 minutes until they are translucent. Remove the prawns from the wok and set aside in a hot place. Add the cod to the wok and stir for 2 minutes. Remove and add the cod to the prawns. Add the lime marinade, fish sauce and chilli. Stir until the liquid is slightly reduced. Pour the liquid over the hot prawns and cod and garnish with spring onions and fresh coriander.

PRAWNS, CORIANDER AND PESTO

These prawns are fabulous – it's the taste of coriander and pesto that makes all the difference. Serve on their own as a starter or with rice for lunch. Serves 4.

45ml/3 tbsp olive oil
12 large green prawns, peeled and deveined, tails left on
60ml/4 tbsp pesto

Small bunch fresh coriander, finely chopped
Salt
Freshly ground black pepper

Heat the wok, add the olive oil and, when the oil is hot and begins to smoke, add the prawns, pesto and coriander. Stir for ½ minute. Lower the heat and stir for 2-3 minutes. Season with salt and freshly ground pepper to taste.

Above: Prawns, Coriander and Pesto

Mussels, Coconut Milk and Lemon Grass

The addition of lemon grass to mussels gives them an exceptional flavour. This is a delicious starter for 6 or can be served as a main meal for 4 when accompanied by brown rice.

1kg/2¼lb fresh mussels
2 lemon grass stalks, cut into 1cm/½in lengths
1 small tin of coconut milk

15ml/1 tbsp fish sauce
50g/2oz small, fresh whole coriander leaves.

Clean the mussels well. Crush the lemon grass to release the flavour.

Heat the wok, add the coconut milk and lemon grass, bring to the boil and allow to simmer and reduce for 3-5 minutes. Increase the heat and add the mussels and the fish sauce, and cover the wok for 1 minute. Then remove the cover and stir well until the mussels open. (Discard any that haven't opened.) Place the mussels in a large serving dish and add a small amount of the coconut milk. Scatter with the coriander leaves to garnish.

Garlic and Chilli Prawns

A fabulous starter or light lunch dish. Fresh coriander adds an extra hint of the Orient to the prawns. Delicious served on their own or with rice. Serves 4.

30ml/2 tbsp groundnut oil
3 garlic cloves, finely chopped
3 red chillies, deseeded and cut into very thin rings
12 large green prawns, peeled and deveined, tails left on

6 sprigs fresh coriander leaves
Salt
Freshly ground black pepper

Heat the wok, add the groundnut oil and, when the oil is very hot and begins to smoke, add the garlic, chillies and prawns. Stir for 5 minutes or until the prawns are pink and cooked. Add the coriander leaves and season with salt and pepper to taste. Stir for 1 minute. Serve.

Stir-Fried Snapper

Serve the snappers on a large plate for maximum effect. Serves 4.

2 Snappers – enough for 4, cleaned and scaled
1 lemon
16 slices fresh ginger
1 garlic clove (per fish), crushed

2 spring onions (white part only — use the green part in the dressing), chopped
4 tbsp fresh coriander, finely chopped
40ml/1½fl oz olive oil
4 sprigs fresh coriander

FOR THE DRESSING
60ml/4 tbsp water
25ml/1½ tbsp light soy sauce
5 thin slices fresh ginger
1 red chilli, deseeded and finely sliced
Grated rind of 1 lemon
1 tbsp coriander, finely chopped

1 tsp pale dry sherry
5 turns of freshly ground black pepper
Pinch of salt
1 spring onion (green stem only), cut into matchsticks

With a very sharp knife, score the skin of the snapper in three shallow strips or a diamond pattern. Stuff each fish with a lemon wedge, a few slices of the ginger, the garlic, spring onions and the finely chopped coriander. Leave the snapper to marinate in olive oil for 15 minutes.

In a jug, mix the ingredients for the dressing and set aside.

Heat the wok, add 15-30ml/1-2 tbsp of the oil used in the marinade and, when it is hot, add the fish and stir carefully for 5-7 minutes until half-cooked. Turn the fish over and stir for 5-7 minutes. When cooked, remove to a warm plate. (Repeat this process depending on the number of fish.) When all the snappers are ready, garnish them with the coriander sprigs and serve with the dressing.

Honey and Cracked Black Pepper Scallops

The distinctive taste of the coriander combines perfectly with the scallops. This is a great starter when served with Lemon Thai Rice (see page 46). Serves 4.

12 scallops, cleaned
60ml/4 tbsp honey
1 tbsp cracked black peppercorns
15ml/1 tbsp hot water

25ml/1½ tbsp groundnut oil
2 tsp fresh ginger, finely chopped
1 tbsp fresh coriander, finely chopped

Marinate the scallops in the honey, black peppercorns and water for 15 minutes. Heat the wok, add the groundnut oil and, when the oil is very hot and begins to smoke, add the ginger and stir for ½ minute. Add the scallops along with the marinade. Stir for 3 minutes. Add the coriander and stir for 2 minutes.

Right: Mussels, Coconut Milk and Lemon Grass

CALAMARI, GARLIC AND BASIL

This method of cooking calamari means it not only tastes good but also looks wonderfully different from the usual calamari rings. Serve the dish with noodles or bok-choy. This will serve 2 as a main meal or 4 as a starter.

450g/1lb calamari, fresh or frozen	15g/½oz fresh basil, roughly chopped
30ml/2 tbsp oyster sauce	½ tsp sea salt
30ml/2 tbsp water	1 small red chilli, deseeded and finely
30ml/2 tbsp groundnut oil	chopped
2 garlic cloves, crushed or finely chopped	Freshly ground black pepper

Split open the calamari and remove the backbone. Lay the calamari flat and trim the wide end of any tough pieces. Pat dry with kitchen paper. Make a small criss-cross pattern all over the upper side – about 1x1cm/½x½in, not cutting right through the flesh. Cut into large pieces about 5x5cm/2x2in.

In a small jug, mix together the oyster sauce and water. Heat the wok, add the groundnut oil and, when the oil is very hot and begins to smoke, add the calamari pieces and stir for 1 minute. (The pieces will fan out and begin to curl up into small tubes.) Add the garlic, basil and salt. Stir for 1 minute or until the calamari turns white. Add the sauce mixture and stir for 1 minute. Stir through the chilli and freshly ground black pepper.

SCALLOPS AND VERMICELLI

The delicious aroma of Pernod and basil cannot be described. A perfect lunch or light supper dish served with a green salad. Serves 4.

12 scallops, cleaned	500ml/17fl oz fish stock
100g/4oz vermicelli (or any thin pasta)	60ml/4 tbsp double cream
15ml/1 tbsp olive oil	60ml/4 tbsp Pernod
2 tbsp fresh basil, finely chopped	

Cut the scallops in half to make two rounds. Cook the vermicelli as directed on packet. Drain it well and add the olive oil and basil. Mix thoroughly and keep hot.

Heat the wok, add the fish stock and allow it to reduce by half. Add the cream and Pernod and stir for ½ minute. Finally add the scallops and stir for 2-3 minutes. Pour carefully over the hot vermicelli.

STIR-FRIED MONKFISH, CUCUMBER AND MUSTARD

I discovered this recipe at one of my favourite restaurants, The George and Dragon at Rowde. As Tim Withers, its creator, says, 'It's a simple recipe but a great combination'. Serves 4.

1 cucumber	FOR THE SAUCE:
Salt	150ml/5fl oz crème fraîche
100-150g/4-5oz monkfish per person	150ml/5fl oz double cream
flour for dusting	1 tbsp wholegrain mustard
Freshly ground black pepper	A few shakes of Tabasco
30-45ml/2-3 tbsp groundnut oil –	
depending on the amount of fish	

Deseed and dice the cucumber, sprinkle it with a little salt and leave for 30 minutes. Then refresh it with cold water and drain.

Prepare the sauce by whisking together the ingredients over a gentle heat until heated through.

Cut the monkfish into even-sized strips and dust them with flour, seasoned with a little salt and pepper.

Heat the wok, add the groundnut oil and, when the oil is very hot and begins to smoke, add the monkfish strips and stir for 1-2 minutes. Add the cucumber and sufficient sauce to coat everything. Let it settle for a few seconds before serving on heated plates.

Right: Calamari, Garlic and Basil

RICE & NOODLES

Whether a main dish or accompaniment, rice and noodles are versatile stir-fry ingredients. They are the ideal partners for rich or spicy sauces, and they give balance and bulk without detracting from the flavour of the dish. Plain white rice or simple egg noodles are best for serving with more complex flavours, or experiment with unusual types such as wild rice or Japanese buckwheat noodles.

FRESH TOMATOES AND NOODLES

The slight sweetness of this dish is delicious. Wonderful on its own, it will also complement fish, meat or poultry. Serves 4.

250g/9oz Chinese egg noodles	*1 tsp brown sugar*
2 tsp walnut oil	*Salt*
300g/11oz ripe tomatoes, peeled, deseeded	*Freshly ground black pepper*
and chopped	*15ml/1 tbsp groundnut oil*
1 heaped tbsp fresh basil, chopped	*3 garlic cloves, crushed*
½ tsp fresh oregano	*50g/2oz leeks, finely chopped*

Cook the noodles as directed on the packet. Drain well and stir through with the walnut oil.

In a bowl, combine the tomatoes, basil, oregano, sugar and salt and pepper.

Heat the wok, add the groundnut oil and, when the oil is very hot and begins to smoke, add the garlic and stir for ½ minute. Add the leeks and stir for 2 minutes. Add the noodles and stir for 2 minutes. Finally add the tomato mixture and stir for 2-3 minutes until the noodles are very hot. Season to taste.

EASY FRIED RICE

This no-nonsense dish is a delicious accompaniment to any meat, fish or poultry dish. Serves 4.

15ml/1 tbsp groundnut oil	*1 tbsp fresh coriander, finely chopped*
1 garlic clove, crushed	*1 small red pepper or chilli, deseeded*
4 spring onions, finely sliced diagonally	*and very finely sliced*
250g/9oz white long grain rice, pre-cooked	*1 tsp sesame oil*
and cooled	*Freshly ground red peppercorns*
Salt	

Heat the wok, add the groundnut oil and, when the oil is very hot and begins to smoke, add the garlic and stir for ½ minute. Add the spring onions and stir for 1 minute, adding the rice and a little salt. Stir for 3 minutes, then add the coriander and stir for 1 minute or until the rice is very hot. Add the red pepper or chilli and stir for 1 minute. Stir through the sesame oil and finish with a light covering of freshly ground red peppercorns.

WILD RICE WITH SUN-DRIED TOMATOES, PARSLEY AND LEMON RIND

Taste-as-you-cook with this dish, as measurements vary according to the amount of rice you are cooking. This is delicious served on its own or as an accompaniment to poultry or fish. Serves 4.

250-350g/9-12oz wild rice	*2 tbsp lemon rind*
60-90ml/4-6 tbsp olive oil	*Salt*
10 sun-dried tomatoes	*Freshly ground black pepper*
5 tbsp parsley, finely chopped	*Parmesan cheese shavings*

Cook the rice following the directions on the packet, as each brand is slightly different. Rinse well and allow to cool.

Heat the wok, add the olive oil and, when the oil is very hot and begins to smoke, add the sun-dried tomatoes and the cooked rice to the wok. Stir for 1-2 minutes, adding the parsley and lemon rind. Season with salt and pepper to taste. Serve with shavings of Parmesan cheese on top.

BROWN LEMON RICE

The lemon myrtle oil makes this rice something really special so it's well worth trying to find it. If you prefer, try using all coriander or all parsley according to your taste. Serves 4.

Juice of 1 lemon, freshly squeezed
Finely grated rind of 1 lemon
1 tsp caster sugar
15ml/1 tbsp groundnut oil
200g/7oz brown rice, pre-cooked and cooled

15ml/1 tbsp light soy sauce
1 tbsp coriander leaves and parsley, chopped
1 tsp lemon myrtle oil
Freshly ground red peppercorns

In a small jug, mix together the lemon juice, rind and caster sugar.

Heat the wok, add the groundnut oil and, when the oil is very hot and begins to smoke, add the rice and stir for 3 minutes. Add the lemon mixture and stir for 2 minutes. Add the soy sauce and stir for 1 minute. Add the coriander and parsley and stir for 2 minutes or until the rice is very hot. Stir through the lemon myrtle oil, finally adding the pepper to taste.

PINEAPPLE RICE

The addition of pineapple gives this super-quick rice recipe an unusual fresh taste. Delicious served with chicken and pork. Serves 4.

4 slices fresh or tinned pineapple
350ml/12fl oz water (only if using fresh pineapple), or juice from the tinned pineapple

250g/9oz long grain white rice
15-30ml/1-2 tbsp groundnut oil

If using fresh pineapple, remove the core and outer skin. Cut it into small chunks and soak in water for 10 minutes. (If using tinned pineapple you only need to cut the pineapple.)

Rinse the rice before cooking. Combine the pineapple juice and cooking water and otherwise proceed as directed on the rice packet.

Heat the wok. Add the groundnut oil and, when the oil is very hot and begins to smoke, add the rice and pineapple cubes. (If the rice sticks, add a little more oil, but the less oil used, the better the taste.) Stir for 2 minutes or until the rice is hot.

LEMON THAI RICE

With its extra lemon tang, this rice makes a perfect accompaniment to fish and seafood dishes. Serves 4.

Freshly grated rind of 1 lemon
Juice of 1 lemon
1-2 tsp caster sugar
30ml/2 tbsp groundnut oil

250g/9oz long grain white rice, pre-cooked and cooled
50g/2oz sultanas
50g/2oz almonds, flaked and roasted

In a small jug, combine the lemon rind with the juice and caster sugar.

Heat the wok, add the groundnut oil and, when the oil is very hot and begins to smoke, add the rice and stir for 1 minute. Add the sultanas, almonds and lemon mixture. Stir for 3 minutes or until the rice is hot.

CHOW MEIN NOODLES

This is a classic recipe and a great family favourite. Substitute any white meat for the chicken to make a change. It's best served with a green salad.

250g/9oz Chinese egg noodles
450g/1lb chicken breast, cut into strips
65g/2½oz plain flour
30ml/2 tbsp groundnut oil
30ml/2 tbsp sesame oil
8 thin slices fresh ginger
2 garlic cloves, crushed
2 spring onions, white parts chopped (use green section for garnish)

400g/14oz small prawns, peeled
100g/4oz peas, fresh or frozen
30ml/2 tbsp oyster sauce

FOR THE SAUCE
150ml/5fl oz chicken stock
1 tbsp cornflour
15ml/1 tbsp light soy sauce

Cook the noodles as directed on the packet. Drain them well and set aside. Toss the chicken in the flour and shake off any excess flour. Combine the sauce ingredients in a jug. Heat the wok, add the groundnut oil and, when the oil is very hot, add the chicken and stir for 3-4 minutes. With a slotted spoon, remove the chicken and pat dry with kitchen paper. Set aside in a warm place.

Wipe out the wok. Now reheat the wok, add the sesame oil and, when the oil is hot, add the ginger, garlic and spring onions. Stir for 1 minute. Add the chicken, prawns, peas and oyster sauce and stir for 2 minutes. Add the sauce mixture and stir for 2 minutes or until it is reduced by a quarter. Add the noodles and stir for 1-2 minutes or until they are hot. Serve topped with the finely chopped green section of the spring onions.

Right: Brown Lemon Rice and Lemon Thai Rice

SWEET AND SOUR NOODLES

Always a favourite combination of flavours, this recipe will be enjoyed by non-vegetarians equally as well as vegetarians. Serves 4.

100g/4oz broccoli
3 tsp cornflour
2 tsp brown sugar
2 tsp tomato sauce
450g/1 lb canned pineapple pieces
1 small red chilli, very finely sliced
250g/9oz Chinese egg noodles
2 tsp sesame oil

45ml/3 tbsp groundnut oil
1 medium red pepper, deseeded and sliced
1 medium green pepper, deseeded and sliced
1 large carrot, peeled and thinly sliced diagonally
150g/5oz button mushrooms, sliced
2 spring onions finely sliced diagonally
1tbsp sesame seeds

Cut broccoli into small florets. Peel and slice the stems diagonally. In a jug combine the cornflour, brown sugar and tomato sauce. Add undrained pineapple and red chilli. Mix well.

Cook noodles in a large saucepan of boiling water for 3-5 minutes. Drain well and stir through sesame oil. This will stop them drying out until ready to use. Set aside.

Heat wok or large pan, add groundnut oil and when the oil is very hot or begins to smoke add the broccoli, peppers, carrot and mushrooms. Stir for 3-4 minutes or until vegetables are tender but still crisp. Add noodles and stir for 2 minutes. Pour in sauce mixture and stir for 4 minutes. Add spring onions and sesame seeds and stir for 1 minute.

BOLOGNESE NOODLES

This is a great alternative to Spaghetti Bolognese. It's so quick and easy and makes a perfect winter lunch dish or a light supper for the whole family. Use whatever pasta or noodles you have in the storecupboard. Serves 4.

250g/9oz Chinese egg noodles
15ml/1 tbsp groundnut oil
2 garlic cloves, crushed
2 onions, roughly chopped
450g/1lb beef mince
2 bay leaves

12 button mushrooms, sliced
3 sprigs thyme
450g/1lb tinned tomatoes
15ml/1 tbsp tomato purée
250ml/8fl oz concentrated tomato soup
Parmesan or Cheddar cheese, grated

Cook the noodles as directed on the packet. Drain them and set aside in a warm place.

Heat the wok, add the groundnut oil. When the oil is very hot and begins to smoke, add the garlic and onions, stirring for 1-2 minutes or until they have turned opaque. Add the beef, bay leaves, mushrooms and thyme. Stir for 5-6 minutes or until cooked. Add the tomatoes, purée and tomato soup. Cook, stirring occasionally, for a further 4-5 minutes. Finally, add the noodles, stir and serve sprinkled with the grated cheese.

BROWN GINGER RICE

An excellent accompaniment to beef and lamb dishes. Remember to wash the rice well before cooking to ensure that all the grains are separated. Serves 4.

15ml/1 tbsp groundnut oil
1 garlic clove, crushed
1 tsp fresh ginger, grated
200g/7oz brown rice, pre-cooked and cooled

15ml/1 tbsp light soy sauce
1 tbsp fresh chives, finely chopped
1 tsp walnut oil

Heat the wok, add the groundnut oil and, when the oil is very hot and begins to smoke, add the garlic and stir for ½ minute. Add the ginger and stir for ½ minute. Add the rice and stir for 3 minutes or until the rice is hot. Add the soy sauce and chives and stir for 1 minute. Finally, stir through the walnut oil.

RED CAMARGUE RICE AND BACON

This new rice, from the Camargue region of southern France, with its distinctive colour not only looks great but also has a delicious nutty flavour. Serves 4.

15ml/1 tbsp groundnut oil
1 garlic clove, crushed
1 tsp fresh ginger, grated
200g/7oz red Camargue rice, pre-cooked and cooled
3 rashers lean bacon, chopped into small cubes

½ green pepper, deseeded and finely chopped
½ yellow or orange pepper, deseeded and finely chopped
15ml/1 tbsp soy sauce

Heat the wok, add the groundnut oil and, when the oil is very hot and begins to smoke, add the garlic and ginger and stir for ½ minute. Add the rice and stir for 2-3 minutes, after which add the bacon and peppers. Stir for 2 minutes, then add the soy sauce. Stir for 3 minutes or until the rice is very hot.

RED CAMARGUE RICE AND GARLIC

This is a delicious accompaniment to meat, poultry and fish dishes or even as a light meal on its own. Serves 4.

15ml/1 tbsp groundnut oil
1 garlic clove, crushed
6 spring onions, finely sliced diagonally
200g/7oz red Camargue rice, pre-cooked and cooled

1 tsp walnut oil
Sea salt
Freshly ground black pepper

Heat the wok, add the groundnut oil and, when the oil is very hot and begins to smoke, add the garlic and stir for ½ minute. Add the spring onions and stir for 1 minute. Add the rice and stir for 3-4 minutes or until the rice is very hot. Stir through the walnut oil for ½ minute. Finally add salt and pepper to taste.

Right: Sweet and Sour Noodles

FRIED RICE COMBINATION

Fried rice is usually cooked with pre-boiled and cooled rice (which can be kept covered in the fridge for up to 4 days). This ensures the grains are dry and separated before the frying process and avoids a gluggy mess. Always serve soy sauce separately or it will discolour the rice if added during cooking. This recipe serves 4 – a good rule is to allow 50g/2oz rice for each person.

15ml/1 tbsp groundnut oil
2 garlic cloves, crushed or finely chopped
200g/7oz long grain white rice,
pre-cooked and cooled
¼ red pepper, deseeded and diced
¼ yellow or orange pepper,
deseeded and diced
50g/2oz button mushrooms, wiped
and sliced

50g/2oz thick rashers bacon or ham
50g/2oz frozen peas, thawed
50g/2oz small prawns, cooked
3 spring onions, finely sliced diagonally
Salt
Freshly ground black pepper

Heat the wok, add the oil and, when the oil is very hot and begins to smoke, add the garlic and stir for ½ minute. Add the rice and stir for 2 minutes. Add the peppers and stir for 1 minute, then add the mushrooms, bacon or ham and peas, stirring for 1 minute. Add the prawns and stir for 1 minute. Finally add the spring onions, salt and pepper to taste, and stir for 1 minute or until the rice is very hot.

BROWN FRIED RICE

The nutty texture of brown rice makes a flavoursome alternative to the traditional white rice accompaniment to dishes. Remember though that brown rice takes twice as long to cook as white. This quantity should serve 4.

30ml/2 tbsp groundnut oil
100g/4oz small button mushrooms, sliced
6 spring onions, finely sliced diagonally
½ medium-sized red pepper, deseeded
and finely diced

½ medium-sized green pepper, deseeded
and finely diced
250g/9oz brown rice, pre-cooked and cooled
15ml/1 tbsp light soy sauce

Heat the wok, add the groundnut oil and, when the oil is very hot and begins to smoke, add the vegetables and stir for 2 minutes. Add the rice and stir for 3-4 minutes or until the vegetables are tender but still crisp. Add the soy sauce and stir for ½ minute or until the rice is hot.

NOODLES AND FRESH HERBS

This tangy, sharp recipe is a meal in itself but it is also an excellent accompaniment to meat and poultry. Serves 4.

250g/9oz Chinese egg noodles
1 tsp + 30ml/2 tbsp basil oil
15ml/1 tbsp groundnut oil
3 garlic cloves, finely chopped
1 small red pepper, very finely chopped
1 heaped tbsp fresh basil, chopped

1 heaped tbsp fresh parsley, chopped
1 tsp fresh tarragon, chopped
Grated rind of ½ lemon
Salt
Citrus pepper

Cook the noodles as directed on the packet. Drain well and stir through with 1 tsp basil oil.

Heat the wok, add the groundnut oil and, when the oil is very hot and begins to smoke, add the garlic and red pepper. Stir for ½ minute. Add the noodles and stir for 2-3 minutes. Add the herbs and lemon rind. Stir for 2 minutes until the noodles are very hot. Add the remaining basil oil and stir for 1 minute, making sure all the noodles are coated with the oil. Season with salt and citrus pepper to taste.

NOODLES, SUN-DRIED TOMATOES AND ASPARAGUS

This is a marvellous summer meal, when fresh asparagus is at its best. Fresh basil is just perfect with prosciutto and sun-dried tomatoes. Use any type of noodle except vermicelli. Serves 4.

4 slices bread, ideally olive or basil bread
Olive oil, for brushing
250g/9 oz Chinese egg noodles
15ml/1 tbsp basil oil
8 asparagus stalks, cut into 4cm/
1½in lengths

12 sun-dried tomatoes
4 slices prosciutto, cut into strips
6 tbsp basil, finely chopped
Parmesan cheese
Freshly ground pepper

Slice the bread into croûton-sized pieces and brush them with olive oil. Place them in the oven on high until golden brown, then remove and allow to cool on kitchen paper.

Cook the noodles as directed on the packet. Drain them and set aside.

Heat the wok or large pan, add the oil and, when the oil is very hot and begins to smoke, add the asparagus. Stir for 3-4 minutes or until nearly cooked. Add the sun-dried tomatoes, prosciutto, basil and noodles, stir for 1 minute. Serve with the croûtons, Parmesan and freshly ground pepper to taste.

Right: Fried Rice Combination

VEGETABLES

Most stir-fry recipes use large amounts of fresh seasonal vegetables. Try unusual Chinese varieties or a combination of old favourites with a new sauce or spices. You will be amazed how good vegetables can taste, how easy they are to cook and how and how well they retain their colour, texture and nutritional value with stir-frying.

STIR-FRIED VEGETABLE FONDUE

This is a great fun-dish for all the family. It is very versatile and any vegetable can be used. The ones listed below are especially good as they do not need to be cooked in advance and they hold their shape. Use whichever combination is to hand to make up the necessary weight. Serves 4-6.

A combined weight of about 450g/1lb vegetables, such as: cherry tomatoes, cauliflower, broccoli, beans, asparagus, peppers, carrots and celery
30ml/2 tbsp olive oil

2 garlic cloves, whole
3 sprigs fresh rosemary
2 tsp salt
10 turns of freshly ground black pepper
300g/11oz Gruyère cheese, grated

Clean and chop the vegetables into appropriate sizes. Heat the wok or large pan, add the olive oil and, when the oil is very hot, add the garlic, rosemary, salt, freshly ground pepper and vegetables, except for the tomatoes (if using), and stir for 4-5 minutes. Add the tomatoes and stir for 1 minute, before removing the rosemary. Place the vegetables in a large hot dish and keep them warm. Heat the cheese in a saucepan or a microwave until runny. (Do not remove the cheese from the saucepan until you are ready to eat as it cools very quickly.) Pour the cheese into a large bowl and serve as the dip for the vegetables.

ASPARAGUS, BROAD BEANS AND MUSHROOMS

The tang of the lemon adds an extra fresh taste to the vegetables without overwhelming their flavours. Serves 4.

2 tsp lemon juice, freshly squeezed
Grated rind of ½ lemon
1 tsp brown sugar
½ tsp citrus or lemon pepper
15ml/1 tbsp groundnut oil
1 garlic clove, crushed or finely chopped

2 rashers lean bacon, chopped
250g/9oz fresh asparagus, sliced diagonally into 4cm/1½in lengths
50g/2oz small broad beans
50g/2oz button mushrooms, sliced

In a small jug, combine the lemon juice, rind, sugar and pepper. Heat the wok, add the oil and, when the oil is very hot and begins to smoke, add the garlic and stir for ½ minute. Add the bacon and stir for 1 minute. Then stir in the asparagus and broad beans for 2 minutes. Add the mushrooms and stir for 2 minutes. Finally, add the lemon juice mixture and stir everything for 2 minutes or until the vegetables are cooked but still crisp.

MANGETOUT, CARROTS AND LIME

These vegetables have a delicious sweet flavour and are good to eat on their own or are a perfect accompaniment to any meat or poultry dish. Serves 4.

15ml/1 tbsp lime juice
Grated rind of 1 lime
1 tsp brown sugar
15ml/1 tbsp groundnut oil

2 garlic cloves, crushed
150g/5oz carrots, finely sliced diagonally
150g/5oz small whole mangetout, trimmed

In a small jug, combine the lime juice, rind and brown sugar. Mix well.

Heat the wok, add the groundnut oil and, when the oil is very hot and begins to smoke, add the garlic and stir for ½ minute. Add the lime mixture and stir for 1 minute. Add the carrots and stir for 2 minutes. Add the mangetout and stir for 2-3 minutes or until the vegetables are cooked but still crisp.

CABBAGE, MUSHROOMS AND BACON

This makes a delicious lunch dish or a side vegetable with more traditional cuts of meat. Serves 4.

30ml/2 tbsp groundnut oil
1 large red onion, finely chopped
50g/2oz bacon, rind removed and finely chopped
2 garlic cloves, crushed or finely chopped

450g/1lb cabbage, a combination of red, white and Savoy, finely shredded
200g/7oz oyster and button mushrooms, sliced
Freshly ground red peppercorns

Heat the wok, add the groundnut oil and, when the oil is very hot and begins to smoke, add the onion and bacon and stir for 4 minutes. Add the garlic and stir for 2 minutes. Add the cabbage and stir well, keeping the cabbage moving around in the pan for 7 minutes. Add the mushrooms and stir for 3 minutes. Season with the pepper to taste.

STIR-FRY TOFU AND VEGETABLES

The creamy texture of the tofu contrasts well with the crisp and crunchy vegetables. Serves 4.

30ml/2 tbsp groundnut oil
1 garlic clove, crushed
2 tsp fresh ginger, grated
Dash of paprika
30ml/2 tbsp dark soy sauce
225g/8oz tofu, cut into 2.5cm/1in squares
2 sprigs rosemary
1 medium-sized red pepper, deseeded and cut into 2.5cm/1in squares

1 medium-sized green pepper, deseeded and cut into 2.5cm/1in squares
175g/6oz courgettes, sliced diagonally
3 spring onions, thinly sliced
100g/4oz bamboo shoots, drained
100g/4oz shiitake mushrooms, sliced
Pinch of Chinese five spice
Freshly ground black pepper
15ml/1 tbsp pale dry sherry

Heat the wok, add 15ml/1 tbsp groundnut oil and, when the oil is very hot and begins to smoke, add the garlic and 1 tsp ginger. Stir for ½ minute. Add the paprika and 15ml/1 tbsp soy sauce. Stir for ½ minute. Add the tofu and stir for 3 minutes. With a slotted spoon, remove the tofu and set aside in a warm place. Wipe out the wok and reheat it. Add 15ml/1 tbsp groundnut oil and, when the oil is very hot and begins to smoke, add 1 tsp ginger and stir for ½ minute. Add the rosemary and vegetables, Chinese five spice and black pepper to taste. Stir for 3 minutes. Add the sherry and 15ml/1 tbsp soy sauce and stir for 2 minutes. Return the tofu to the wok and stir for 2-3 minutes until hot. Remove the rosemary before serving.

OKRA AND TOMATOES

Wipe rather than wash okra or it will become too slippery to cook with. Serves 4.

15ml/1 tbsp groundnut oil
1 garlic clove, crushed or finely chopped
1 medium-sized onion, finely sliced
450g/1lb okra, trimmed and cut into 2.5cm/1in lengths

450g/1lb yellow or red tomatoes, skinned, deseeded and chopped
Salt
Freshly ground black pepper
1 tbsp fresh coriander, chopped (optional)

Heat the wok, add the groundnut oil and, when the oil is very hot and begins to smoke, add the garlic and stir for ½ minute. Add the onion and stir for 2 minutes or until it is soft but not browned. Add the okra, tomatoes, and salt and pepper to taste. Stir for 3-4 minutes until the okra is cooked but still crisp. Stir through the chopped coriander (if using) and serve.

MUSHROOMS, BEANS AND RED PEPPER

This is a wonderfully colourful vegetable dish that's something different to serve with more conventional cuts of meat and poultry. Serves 4.

15ml/1 tbsp groundnut oil
1 garlic clove, crushed or finely chopped
450g/1lb French beans, sliced diagonally into 4cm/1½ in lengths
½ red pepper, deseeded and cut into 2.5cm/1in squares or diamonds

100g/4oz small button mushrooms, halved
2 tsp sesame oil

Heat the wok, add the groundnut oil and, when the oil is very hot and begins to smoke, add the garlic and stir for ½ minute. Add the beans and red pepper and stir for 2 minutes. Add the mushrooms and stir for 2 minutes or until the vegetables are tender but still crisp. Add the sesame oil and stir for ½ minute.

Right: Cabbage, Mushrooms and Bacon

Above: Bok-choy, Garlic and Oyster Sauce

BOK-CHOY, GARLIC AND OYSTER SAUCE

You should be able to buy bok-choy from Chinese supermarkets but, if you can't find any, try substituting Swiss chard, spinach beet or spinach. Serves 4.

15ml/1 tbsp water
30ml/2 tbsp oyster sauce
1 tsp brown sugar
15ml/1 tbsp groundnut oil
2 garlic cloves, finely chopped

250g/9oz green bok-choy, washed and well
drained, hard ends removed and each
leaf cut into 4-5 strips
Diced fresh chilli (optional)

In a small jug, mix together the water, oyster sauce and brown sugar and set aside.

Heat the wok, add the oil and, when the oil is very hot and begins to smoke, add the garlic and stir for ½ minute. Add all of the bok-choy and stir for 2 minutes. Now add the sauce mixture and chilli, if using, and stir for 1 minute. Be very careful not to overcook this dish as the bok-choy should still be crispy when served.

AUBERGINE, TOMATOES AND CHINESE MUSHROOMS

Salting aubergines may seem out of fashion but this process does keep them from absorbing moisture during cooking, resulting in a less soggy dish. Serves 4.

4 dried Chinese mushrooms
450g/1 lb aubergines, cubed
250g/9oz tomatoes
About 30ml/2 tbsp groundnut oil
2 garlic cloves, crushed

15ml/1 tbsp soy sauce
2 spring onions, sliced
Salt
Freshly ground black pepper

Soak the dried mushrooms in boiling water for 15-20 minutes to soften, then pat dry and slice thinly. Sprinkle the aubergines with salt and let stand for 20 minutes. Rinse well with cold water and pat dry with kitchen towels.

Meanwhile, plunge the tomatoes into boiling water for 1 minute to soften the skin. Peel, deseed and chop coarsely.

Heat a wok or large pan and add the oil. When it is hot and beginning to smoke, add the garlic and stir for 30 seconds. Add the aubergine and stir for 6-7 minutes, adding more oil if necessary. Add the mushrooms and tomatoes and str for 2 minutes. Add the soy sauce and stir for 1 minute. Add the spring onion and stir for 1 minute. Season with salt and pepper.

CARROTS, COURGETTES AND WATERCRESS

This is a quick and easy combination which makes a great accompaniment to poultry or any meat dish. Serves 4.

15ml/1 tbsp groundnut oil
200g/7oz carrots, cut into sticks 5cm/2in
long and 1cm/½in thick
200g/7oz courgettes, cut as the carrots

4 spring onions, chopped diagonally
15ml/1 tbsp light soy sauce
1 bunch watercress
2 tsp sesame seeds, roasted

Heat the wok, add the groundnut oil and, when the oil is very hot and begins to smoke, add the carrots and stir for 1 minute. Add the courgettes and spring onions and stir for 2-3 minutes or until the vegetables are tender but still crisp. Add the soy sauce and watercress and stir for 1 minute. Stir through the sesame seeds, leaving a few to sprinkle on the top.

WARM MUSHROOM SALAD

Good on its own or as a scrumptious side salad with beef or lamb.
Serves 4.

250g/9oz mixed salad leaves and baby
spinach
25g/1oz fresh mint, roughly chopped
25g/2oz butter
2 garlic cloves, crushed
250-300g/9-11oz mixed mushrooms,
halved

FOR THE DRESSING
30ml/2 tbsp balsamic vinegar
150ml/5fl oz olive oil
1 tsp mango chutney
Salt
Freshly ground black pepper

In a large bowl, combine the salad leaves, spinach and mint. Make the
dressing, but do not add to the salad until the mushrooms are cooked.

Heat the wok to a medium-high heat, and add the butter and garlic.
Stir for 1 minute. Add the mushrooms and stir for 4 minutes or until
cooked. Add the dressing to the salad. With a slotted spoon, remove
the mushrooms from the wok and place them on the bed of salad.
Season with salt and pepper to taste.

VEGETARIAN STIR-FRY WITH FRESH HERBS

Just as good to eat as it looks. Serves 4.

25ml/1½ tbsp groundnut oil
100g/4oz mixed red, green and orange
peppers, deseeded and cut into
3cm/1 ¼in strips
100g/4oz carrots, cut into julienne strips
100g/4oz runner beans, cut into
3cm/1¼in strips
100g/4oz fresh asparagus tips, cut
diagonally into 3 cm/1 ¼in strips

100g/4oz mangetout, sliced diagonally
and cut into 3cm/1¼in pieces
3 spring onions, sliced diagonally
1 tbsp fresh basil, finely chopped
1 tbsp fresh parsley, finely chopped
½ tsp lemon juice
1 tsp basil oil
Salt
Freshly ground black pepper

Heat the wok, add the groundnut oil and, when the oil is very hot and
begins to smoke, add the peppers, carrots, beans, asparagus and
mangetout, in that order. Stir for 4-5 minutes. Add the spring onions,
basil and parsley and stir for 1 minute or until the vegetables are
cooked but still crisp. Add the lemon juice and stir for ½ minute. Add
the basil oil and stir for 1 minute. Season to taste.

BROCCOLI, RED PEPPER AND PINE NUTS

No one will believe that these wonderful nutty and aromatic tastes
have been so fabulously simple to create. Serves 4.

30ml/2 tbsp fish sauce
30ml/2 tbsp water
2 tsp brown sugar
30ml/2 tbsp groundnut oil
450g/1lb broccoli, cut into small florets,
stems sliced diagonally
1 medium-sized red pepper, deseeded
and diced

6 spring onions, sliced
25g/1oz fresh coriander leaves, roughly
chopped
2 tsp sesame oil
65g/2½oz pine nuts, roasted

In a small jug, combine the fish sauce, water and brown sugar.

Heat the wok, add the groundnut oil and, when the oil is very hot and
begins to smoke, add the broccoli. Stir for 1 minute. Add the red
pepper, spring onions and coriander leaves and stir for 2 minutes. Add
the fish sauce mixture and stir for 2-3 minutes or until the broccoli is
tender but still crisp. Finally, stir through the sesame oil and pine nuts.
Serve immediately.

Above: Broccoli, Red Pepper and Pine Nuts

57

BRUSSELS SPROUTS AND WALNUTS

A delicious and unusual twist to an everyday vegetable. Excellent with roasted or grilled meat. Serves 4.

30ml/2 tbsp groundnut oil
1 garlic clove, finely chopped or crushed
1 tsp fresh ginger, grated
450g/1lb small Brussels sprouts, whole or halved

30ml/2 tbsp light soy sauce
100g/4oz walnuts, roasted and halved or in large pieces
1 tsp walnut oil

Heat the wok, add the groundnut oil and, when the oil is very hot and begins to smoke, add the garlic and ginger. Stir for ½ minute. Add the sprouts and stir for 3 minutes. Add the soy sauce and walnuts and stir for 4-5 minutes, or until the sprouts are cooked but still crisp. Add the walnut oil and stir for ½ minute.

MIXED MUSHROOMS WITH GARLIC AND HERBS

This is a stir-fried version of a perennial favourite. Use any type of fresh herbs you fancy but they must be fresh – dried simply will not do. You can stir in a knob of butter just before serving for a richer flavour. Serves 4.

30ml/2 tbsp groundnut oil
700g/1½lb mixed mushrooms, including shiitake, brown, oyster and button, thinly sliced
1-2 garlic cloves, crushed

Several sprigs each fresh herbs, such as chervil, tarragon, parsley and basil, leaves chopped
Salt
Freshly ground black pepper

Heat the wok, add the groundnut oil and, when the oil is very hot and begins to smoke, add the mushrooms. Stir for 2-3 minutes until just cooked. Add the garlic and stir for 1 minute. Add the herbs and stir just to cook through. Serve immediately.

CAULIFLOWER, PECAN NUTS AND CORIANDER

A great twist to a standard vegetable. To make a change, serve it with a grill or roast. Serves 4.

30ml/2 tbsp water
15ml/1 tbsp pale dry sherry
15ml/1 tbsp light soy sauce
15ml/1 tbsp groundnut oil
2 garlic cloves, finely chopped or crushed

450g/1lb cauliflower, cut into florets
2 spring onions, finely sliced diagonally
50g/2oz pecan nuts, halved or in large pieces
1 tsp sesame oil

In a small jug, combine the water, sherry and soy sauce. Heat the wok, add the groundnut oil and, when the oil is very hot and begins to smoke, add the garlic and stir for ½ minute. Add the cauliflower and stir for 2-3 minutes. Add the spring onions and stir for 2 minutes. Add the sauce mixture and stir for 2 minutes. Add the nuts and stir for 2 minutes or until the cauliflower is cooked but still crisp. Stir through the sesame oil.

TOMATOES AND HERBS

If you can't find yellow pear tomatoes, use all cherry tomatoes instead. Swap the suggested herbs for whichever ones you prefer. Try mint instead of chives for a change. Serves 4.

15ml/1 tbsp groundnut oil
2 garlic cloves, crushed or finely chopped
250g/9oz cherry tomatoes
250g/9oz yellow pear tomatoes

1 heaped tbsp fresh basil, chopped
1 heaped tbsp fresh chives, finely chopped
Salt
Freshly ground black pepper

Heat the wok, add the groundnut oil and, when the oil is very hot and begins to smoke, add the garlic and stir for 1 minute. Add the tomatoes and stir for 2 minutes. Add the herbs and stir for 2 minutes or until the tomatoes are hot. (Be careful not to allow the tomatoes to become too soft – keep them moving around the pan.) Add the salt and freshly ground black pepper to taste.

Right: Brussel Sprouts and Walnuts, and Cauliflower, Pecan Nuts and Coriander

Vegetable Stir-Fry

Always slice the vegetables diagonally as this allows more of the surface of them to come into contact with the heat, and so cooks them faster. This dish is a meal in itself. Serves 4.

30ml/2 tbsp groundnut oil
1 garlic clove, finely chopped
2 tsp fresh ginger, grated
200g/7oz broccoli, cut into florets, stems sliced diagonally
200g/7oz beans, cut into 4cm/1 ½in lengths diagonally
1 medium-sized red pepper, deseeded and cut into strips
1 medium-sized yellow pepper, deseeded and cut into strips
150g/5oz button mushrooms, halved

2 spring onions, sliced
100g/3oz bean sprouts
1 medium courgette, quartered lengthways and sliced
2 celery stalks, cut into 4cm/1½ in lengths on the diagonal
10-12 black olives, pitted
65g/2½oz pine nuts, roasted
2 tsp soy sauce
15ml/1 tbsp sesame oil
Freshly ground black pepper
Salt

Heat the wok, add the groundnut oil and, when the oil is very hot and begins to smoke, add the garlic and ginger. Stir for 1 minute. Add the broccoli and beans and stir for 1 minute. Add remaining vegetables, the olives and half the pine nuts. Stir for 2 minutes or until the vegetables are tender but still crisp. Stir through the soy sauce and sesame oil for 1 minute. Season to taste with salt and pepper and sprinkle with the remaining pine nuts.

Courgettes, Tomatoes and Garlic

This exceptionally quick and easy dish will jazz up a simple meat or poultry dish. Serves 4.

15ml/1 tbsp groundnut oil
2 garlic cloves, finely chopped
450g/1lb courgettes, sliced diagonally into 2cm/1in lengths

200g/7oz small tomatoes, about 50g/2oz each, halved
Salt
Freshly ground black pepper

Heat the wok, add the groundnut oil and, when the oil is very hot and begins to smoke, add the garlic and stir for ½ minute. Add the courgettes and stir for 2 minutes. Add the tomatoes and stir for 2-3 minutes or until the vegetables are tender but still crisp. Season with salt and freshly ground pepper to taste.

Spinach with Garlic

Spinach is regaining favour as a vegetable. This looks-good, tastes-good recipe proves why. Serves 4.

15ml/1 tbsp groundnut oil
2 garlic cloves, finely chopped
2 rashers lean bacon, finely sliced

450g/1lb spinach or Swiss chard
2 tbsp pine nuts, roasted

Heat the wok, add the groundnut oil and, when the oil is very hot and begins to smoke, add the garlic and stir for ½ minute. Add the bacon and stir for 2 minutes until the bacon is nearly crisp. Add the spinach or Swiss chard and stir for 3 minutes or until the spinach has wilted. Finally, add the pine nuts and stir for 2 minutes.

Right: Vegetable Stir-Fry

RECIPE INDEX

Mexican-style Chicken Wings 28
monkfish:
    Stir-fried Monkfish, Cucumber
      and Mustard 42
mushrooms:
    Asparagus, Broad Beans and
      Mushrooms 52
    Aubergine, Tomatoes and
      Chinese Mushrooms 56
    Beef, Olives and Mushrooms 28
    Bolognese Noodles 48
    Cabbage, Mushrooms and
      Bacon 54
    Calves Liver and Mushrooms 16
    Chicken, Mushrooms and Basil 30
    Garlic Cream Chicken with
      Oyster Mushrooms 30
    Mixed Mushrooms with Garlic
      and Herbs 58
    Mushrooms, Beans and Red
      Pepper 54
    Stir-fried Quail with Quail Eggs
      and Oyster Mushrooms 20
    Veal, Mushrooms and Garlic 14
    Warm Mushroom Salad 57
Mussels, Coconut Milk and Lemon
* Grass* 40
Mustard, Stir-fried Monkfish,
* Cucumber and* 42
Navarian Lamb 14

noodles:
    Beef, Lettuce and Noodles 12
    Bolognese Noodles 48
    Chow Mein Noodles 46
    Curried Noodles and Quails
      Eggs 18
    Duck and Noodles in Soup 16
    Fresh Tomatoes and Noodles 44
    Noodles and Fresh Herbs 50
    Noodles, Sun-dried Tomatoes
      and Asparagus 50
    Sweet and Sour Noodles 48
Okra and Tomatoes 54

olives:
    Beef, Olives and Mushrooms 28
    Pork and Black Olives 27
oranges:
    Citrus Beef 32
    Citrus Pork and Vegetables 30
    Duck and Orange 14
    Turkey with Citrus-Cranberry
      Sauce 34
oyster sauce:
    Bok-choy, Garlic and Oyster
      Sauce 56
    Pork, Broccoli and Oyster
      Sauce 19
pans 7

parsley:
    Wild Rice with Sun-Dried
      Tomatoes, Parsley and Lemon
      Rind 44
pasta:
    Scallops and Vermicelli 42
pecan nuts:
    Cauliflower, Pecan Nuts and
      Coriander 58
peppercorns:
    Honey and Cracked Black
      Pepper Scallops 40
peppers (sweet):
    Broccoli, Red Pepper and Pine
      Nuts 57
    Lemon Chicken and Sweet
      Peppers 22
    Mushrooms, Beans and Red
      Pepper 54
Pesto, Prawns, Coriander and 39
Pine Nuts, Broccoli, Red Pepper
* and* 57
pineapple:
    Pineapple Beef 22
    Pineapple Rice 46
plum sauce:
    Duck in Plum Sauce 34
    Lamb with Plum Sauce 28
pork:
    Citrus Pork and Vegetables 30
    Honeyed Pork 18
    Pork with Asparagus and Black
      Bean Sauce 34
    Pork and Black Olives 27
    Pork, Broccoli and Oyster
      Sauce 19
    Pork and Lychee Curry 12
    Spicy Pork with Apples 24
    Sweet and Sour Pork 16
prawns:
    Cod and Prawns in Lime Sauce 39
    Garlic and Chilli Prawns 40
    Prawns, Coriander and Pesto 39
    Prawns and Mango 36
Prawns, Scallops, Mangetout and
* Ginger* 38

quail:
    Garlic quail and Vegetables 27
    Stir-fried Quail with Quail Eggs
      and Oyster Mushrooms 20
quails eggs:
    Curried Noodles and Quails
      Eggs 18
    Stir-fried Quail with Quail Eggs
      and Oyster Mushrooms 20
Red Camargue Rice and Bacon 48
Red Camargue Rice and Garlic 48
Red Chicken Curry 27

redcurrant jelly:
    Redcurrant Jelly Lamb 22
    Turkey, Redcurrant Jelly and
      Mint 20
rice:
    Brown Fried Rice 50
    Brown Ginger Rice 48
    Brown Lemon Rice 46
    Easy Fried Rice 44
    Fried Rice Combination 50
    Lemon Thai Rice 46
    Pineapple Rice 46
    Red Camargue Rice and Bacon 48
    Red Camargue Rice and Garlic 48
    Wild Rice with Sun-Dried
      Tomatoes, Parsley and Lemon
      Rind 44

salads:
    Tuna and Guacamole Salad 38
    Warm Chicken Salad 19
    Warm Mushroom Salad 57
Salt and Pepper Squid 36
scallops:
    Honey and Cracked Black
      Pepper Scallops 40
    Prawns, Scallops, Mangetout
      and Ginger 38
    Scallops and Vermicelli 42
Smoked Fish with Vegetables 39
Snapper, Stir-fried 40
Spicy Mango Beef 14
Spicy Pork with Apples 24
Spinach with Garlic 60
Squid, Salt and Pepper 36
storecupboard 5
sugarsnaps:
    Lamb, Sugarsnaps and Mint 16
sweet peppers see peppers
Sweet and Sour Noodles 48
Sweet and Sour Pork 16

tofu:
    Stir-fry Tofu and Vegetables 54
tomatoes:
    Aubergine, Tomatoes and
      Chinese Mushrooms 56
    Courgettes, Tomatoes and
      Garlic 60
    Fresh Tomatoes and Noodles 44
    Okra and Tomatoes 54
    Tomatoes and Herbs 58
    Veal, Tomatoes, Leeks and Basil
      32
tomatoes (sun-dried):
    Noodles, Sun-dried Tomatoes
      and Asparagus 50
    Wild Rice with Sun-Dried
      Tomatoes, Parsley and Lemon
      Rind 44

tomatoes (tinned):
    Bolognese Noodles 48
    Veal, Aubergine and Tomatoes 20
Tuna and Guacamole Salad 38
turkey:
    Turkey with Citrus-Cranberry
      Sauce 34
    Turkey, Redcurrant Jelly and
      Mint 20
    Turkey with Water Chestnuts and
      Choi Sum 22
utensils 7-8

veal:
    Lemon Veal 28
    Veal, Aubergine and Tomatoes 20
    Veal and Lime Curry 19
    Veal, Mushrooms and Garlic 14
    Veal, Tomatoes, Leeks and Basil
      32
vegetables:
    Chicken and Vegetables 26
    Citrus Lamb and Vegetables 24
    Citrus Pork and Vegetables 30
    Garlic Quail and Vegetables 27
    Stir-fried Vegetable Fondue 52
    Stir-fry Tofu and Vegetables 54
    Vegetable Stir-fry 60
    Vegetarian Stir Fry 57
Vermicelli, Scallops and 42

water chestnuts:
    Chicken, Water Chestnuts,
      Asparagus and Black Bean
      Sauce 32
    Turkey with Water Chestnuts
      and Choi Sum 22
Watercress, Carrots, Courgettes
* and* 56
Wild Rice with Sun-Dried Tomatoes,
* Parsley and Lemon Rind* 44
woks 7

ACKNOWLEDGEMENTS

I would like to thank Susan Haynes and Laura Washburn at Weidenfeld & Nicolson for all the support and help they have given me throughout this project. A special thank you to Clare Haynes for her enthusiastic support with testing, typing and inspirational contributions to this book. Thanks also to Fruzzina and Justine Mainwaring, Nicholas Beechey, Janet Payne and Tim Withers. To the staff at 3d Computer Systems, Chippenham for saving my sanity and the future of my new computer. Last but not least, my sincere thanks to Michael Burton for his enduring support throughout this book and for encouraging me to "wok around the clock".

Text Copyright © Weidenfeld & Nicolson 1997

Photographs © Robin Matthews 1997

First published in 1997 by

George Weidenfeld and Nicolson Limited

The Orion Publishing Group

Orion House

5 Upper St. Martin's Lane

London WC2H 9EA

British Library Cataloguing-in-Publication Data

A catalogue record for this book is available from the British Library.

ISBN 0-297-82213-6

Stylist: Roisin Nield

Home Economist: Emma Patmore

Designed by Paul Cooper